ELEVATE & EMPOWER

INSIGHTS ON ENTREPRENEURSHIP, INNOVATION, AND SUCCESS

FEATURING
10 INSPIRING
BUSINESS LEADERS

PROMINENCE
PUBLISHING

This is book 2 in the *Elevate & Empower* series.

Published by Prominence Publishing

www.Prominencepublishing.com

ISBN: 978-1-997649-15-1

Table of Contents

Introduction
By Suzanne Doyle-Ingram, Publisher 1

Chapter 1: Overcome Limiting Belief Systems
By Bonnie L. Silver 5

Chapter 2: Overcoming Fear of Failure During Times of Change
By Mark Guidi.. 15

Chapter 3: It Was Never Failure, It Was Fear
By Shree Rego.. 29

Chapter 4: What Is 'Real' Anymore?
By Dr. Brian Grossman... 41

Chapter 5: Balancing Data Analytics With Intuitive Wisdom
for Optimum Results
By Roben Graziadei, MA.. 59

Chapter 6: Breakthrough Presence: Why Your Next Level
Requires a Shift in How You Show Up
By Victor Bullara, Certified Master Coach...................................... 71

Chapter 7: Leading Change Through Possibility, Purpose,
and People
By Jen Robertson-Hatanaka 85

Chapter 8: Beyond Coaching: How My Business Found Its True
Calling (and How Yours Can Too!)
By Paul Cecala, GCDF 95

Chapter 9: The Exit—What Success Looks Like
By Tony Beebe.. 107

Chapter 10: Why Your Story Matters (And Why the World
Needs to Hear It)
    By Gregg Gonzales 123

Conclusion 131

Introduction

By Suzanne Doyle-Ingram, Publisher

Building a business rarely follows a straight line. It is loops, leaps, and lessons. That is why this anthology exists. Within these pages, ten accomplished leaders open the door to their playbooks and share the ideas, stories, and tools that helped them navigate uncertainty and turn insight into results. The promise is simple: elevate your thinking and empower your next move.

We begin with the work beneath the work. In Chapter 1, **Bonnie L. Silver** invites you to move from wanting to creating by becoming AWARE of limiting beliefs, making the SHIFT, and KNOWing you control what you think and choose next. It is a practical inner toolkit designed to unlock momentum before you change a single tactic.

In Chapter 2, **Mark Guidi** reframes fear of failure during times of change. He shows how progress begins when leaders accept that failure is public and inevitable, then learn from it and keep moving with clarity and courage.

Chapter 3 shifts from outcomes to origins. **Shree Rego** makes a compelling case that mindset is the real CEO of any venture and that inner work is the lever that turns setbacks into comebacks.

In Chapter 4, **Dr. Brian Grossman** asks a timely question: what does it mean to be real when algorithms can imitate almost everything. He offers a daily practice of authenticity that helps readers reclaim agency in an age of artificial everything.

Action meets discernment in Chapter 5. **Roben Graziadei, MA** argues for balancing data analytics with intuitive wisdom. From cockpit instruments to boardroom decisions, she shows how pairing metrics with trained intuition leads to confident execution and measurable wins.

In Chapter 6, **Victor Bullara** illustrates the importance of executive presence and how it affects how others experience your confidence, clarity, and energy in every interaction, both verbal and nonverbal. He writes that executive presence is the ability to project credibility and authenticity, even when you're uncertain.

Chapter 7 centers on how leaders show up and how leaders manage change in a volatile world. **Jen Robertson-Hatanaka** leads change through possibility, purpose, and people, reminding us that your team remembers not only what you did, but how you made them feel in uncertain moments.

In Chapter 8, **Paul Cecala** pulls back the curtain on building a business around passion. He shares how aligning work with what you love can become a sustainable, income-generating practice that elevates clients and owners alike.

Chapter 9 redefines the exit. **Tony Beebe** shares founder stories that highlight purpose beyond the paycheck and offers simple lessons learned from the messy middle to the moment of letting go.

We close in Chapter 10 with **Gregg Gonzales**, who champions the power of personal storytelling. He shows how honest, sometimes humorous stories build trust, spark change, and remind us that our voice belongs in the world.

Throughout the book, you will notice a pattern: Personal truth fuels professional traction. Whether you are releasing a limiting belief, learning to lead through fear, reclaiming what is real, or combining metrics with instinct, each author pairs experience with takeaways you can apply right away. This mix of lived examples and practical next steps is the thread that ties their contributions together.

How to use this book:

- Read one chapter, then choose one small action you will take within the next seven days. Small, consistent moves beat big intentions.

- Share an idea with a colleague or your team. Teaching something once helps you remember it when the pressure is on.

- Revisit chapters as your context changes. What you skim today may become the missing piece six months from now.

As with any anthology, each voice is distinct. The views are those of the individual authors, and part of the value is hearing different angles on the same challenges. Let the variety work for you. Notice what resonates, try what is useful, and adapt it to your world.

Thank you for trusting these leaders with your attention. May their stories and strategies help you build a business that is not only more successful, but also more aligned with who you are and how you want to lead. And remember, the goal here is not to collect ideas. The goal is to convert one idea into action today.

To your success,

Suzanne Doyle-Ingram

Prominence Publishing, Inc.

Chapter 1

Overcome Limiting Belief Systems

There is one grand lie—that we are limited.
The only limits we have are the limits we believe.
~ Wayne Dyer

By Bonnie L. Silver

There was a time in my life when I wanted more for myself. I wanted more customers, more money, more success, better relationships. Have you ever felt that way? The problem is I was "wanting" and not really "creating or making space" for more customers, more money, more success, or healthier relationships. What do I mean by this? Well, when we want something, we tend to keep it at bay. It stays in the desired category, not the accomplished category. The place of perpetual want. When we become aware that the word 'want' is a negative word and that never really gets us to the goals we desire, then we can shift accordingly.

It took me really doing the deep dive within and facing my shadows to acknowledge where I needed to show up for myself. I found it easy to show up for everyone else. Being on the back burner, per se, was my comfort zone. It was comfortable to accept what I was getting without questioning why I wasn't getting more. I didn't really grow,

5

expand, and receive until I stepped out of my comfort zone into complete and utter discomfort. I truly believe we don't really attain all we desire in the comfort zone, but in the discomfort zone.

One of my biggest hurdles of discomfort was back in 2020 when I lived in Southern California, a mile from the ocean. I was in a two-and-a-half-year-long relationship, I was booking bands, going to the beach every day, living my life. In many ways, I was settling for mediocrity. I wasn't fulfilled with my life overall. I felt the pull and nudge that I had to move, buy land, redefine my life, and create anew. Mind you, I had no idea what that really looked like; I just knew things had to change. Big things and big change. My limiting beliefs and existence were no longer going to keep me from the life that I deserved and desired. It was time to really show up for myself. Time to step outside my comfort zone and into the complete unknown, where my new circumstances were going to be so uncomfortable in every way.

So, I did it. I packed up and moved from Southern California, from the 'merely existing' life that I had been living, to South Dakota. Within months of my becoming AWARE, I then made the SHIFT, and I KNEW that this was meant to be.

After creating upheaval in my life in every aspect, I finally settled into my new surroundings. Within a few years, I bought land, met my husband, and created a life and lifestyle that was all new to me, from beekeeping to gardening to having chickens. I redefined my business and my offerings. I learned to live off the land. All aspects of my life have improved. I went from living in mediocrity to living in fulfillment and abundance in all areas.

Most people don't realize that 'want' is actually a limiting belief word. Its literal definition as a verb is to desire or wish for, and as a noun, it is a lack or deficiency. The word want is the opposite of actually 'having' or 'attaining.' How often do we use the word want or hear it used around us?

Most, if not all of us, have some limiting beliefs. A limiting belief is a belief that limits our true potential. They are the negative or fear-based thoughts that hinder us. They are negative words that, when repeated over and over, become the limiting beliefs that keep us wanting but not really getting.

Limiting beliefs can come from a myriad of experiences and projections. They can be around guilt, not feeling worthy, or not feeling deserving, and can keep us from being successful, having financial freedom, and having healthy relationships. These limiting beliefs are the rotten apples that literally ruin everything.

Are limiting beliefs keeping you from becoming a thriving entrepreneur, being successful overall, or even being in that healthy relationship that you know you deserve?

Some limiting beliefs are projected onto us as children from parents, grandparents, friends, etc. Some are self-induced from our own lack of self-worth or personal experiences that we allow to run our lives from childhood, and well into adulthood.

The problem (and solution) is that whatever limiting beliefs we established at a younger age tend to rule us throughout our lifetime. BUT, the great news is we can change! We can shift these limiting beliefs and take our power back. Mold our futures. Create the life we truly desire and deserve.

The key is that we cannot change anything that we don't recognize, so the old adage "Awareness is Key" is tantamount. Becoming aware of these limiting thought patterns is the first step. We are always our worst enemy and the ONLY ones truly holding ourselves back.

In this chapter, I will ask you to do the following: Become AWARE of your limiting beliefs, SHIFT those limiting beliefs, and KNOW that you are in control of what you think and believe.

You will then take that knowledge and be diligent in identifying your patterns going forward. Your new insights will help you create new thought patterns and belief systems that support you and your goals.

Now, let's dive in...

Some limiting beliefs can lie dormant and not rear their ugly heads until you start feeling success or happiness in various areas of life. Then the limiting belief(s) will cause you to self-sabotage. You know what that is all about, right? That's when things are going too well, and instead of "waiting for the other shoe to drop," we create chaos or disruption, usually under the guise of us feeling in control, when actually, the opposite is true. Does this sound familiar?

Are you currently AWARE of what limiting beliefs are holding you back? Let's take a moment and do a quick inventory of different areas and aspects of your life.

Money: Does your bank account stay at a certain number? Can you not figure out why you aren't getting past that threshold? What limiting beliefs do you have around money? Some common negative beliefs include: Money is the root of all evil, money isn't that important, money can't buy happiness, I have to work hard to get money, or another one is that the rich get richer and the poor get poorer. Any of these sound familiar?

Relationships: Do you find it hard to experience healthy, loving relationships? What limiting beliefs do you have around relationships? Here are a few common negative beliefs: I'm not worthy of love, I have to sacrifice for love, I don't trust men/women, there are no quality men/women in my area, etc. Can you relate to any of these negative beliefs?

Health/Fitness: Do you struggle with your health, weight, or overall fitness? What limiting beliefs do you recognize around health and fitness? Again, here are a few common ones so see which of these you believe: I am not athletic, I can't lose weight, I don't have time, I don't like to work out, I'm too old to work out, I like junk food too much.

After taking inventory, think of a time in any one of these areas where you have self-sabotaged in your life and how it may still be impacting you today. Are you ready to shift and let those limiting beliefs and fear-induced mechanisms go?

"Whether You Think You Can,
or Think You Can't... You're Right"
- Henry Ford

Now that you are aware of your limiting beliefs, let's work on the SHIFT of these limiting beliefs.

It's all in our thinking and wording. Take one of your limiting beliefs in one of the categories above and swap out the negative aspect and make it a positive. For example, in lieu of "Money is the root of all evil," make the SHIFT to "Money is the root of all joy" or in lieu of "I'm not worthy of love," make the SHIFT to "I AM worthy of love" or in lieu of "I like junk food too much," make the SHIFT to "I love eating healthy and nutritious foods."

We all have what are called neural pathways. These are the physical connections and networks within our brains that represent and facilitate our thoughts, feelings, and behaviors. These pathways are formed and strengthened through repetition, similar to how a well-trodden path in the ground becomes easier to travel with repeated use. This process, known as neuroplasticity, allows our brain to adapt and change throughout our lives by creating new pathways or strengthening existing ones in response to our experiences, learning, and thoughts. Therefore, it is imperative that you make a conscious and concerted effort continually to shift your thoughts. You have to catch yourself mid-thought or mid-sentence and change your verbiage to the positive. This isn't an overnight task; it will take time. You are literally rewiring your brain by shifting your thoughts and creating new neural pathways.

As I stated early on, I had been accepting living below my best life by being in less than mediocre relationships, low-paying and unfulfilling jobs, and suffering in my health and well-being by not treating my body like the temple that it is. I literally have spent decades rewiring my brain and thought patterns. I have struggled in each area above and still choose to be cognizant of my thoughts while ensuring I stay in a positive verbiage mindset. Focusing on improving my self-esteem and increasing my self-worth at every turn.

Doing the work is never easy. Elevating, rising up, and evolving to become empowered—personally and professionally—takes work and effort. We need to let go of what we 'want' and get clear on what we desire, without the limiting beliefs. Our growth isn't always about the external aspects of making more money or getting more customers. It's the inside job of becoming aligned with ourselves. When we ASK (become AWARE, make the SHIFT, and KNOW our power) ourselves the tough questions and face the tough answers, that is the secret sauce. That is when we become aligned.

Alignment is our true North, the essence of us. That is when everything flows. Things become more seamless. We still show up and put the time and effort in, but it just gets easier. Life is easier. When life becomes easier. We feel less angst, less stressed, less hiccups, and less negativity showing up in our lives.

We then attract the life we desire in all aspects, including money, relationships, health and fitness, and all other aspects of our lives. At this juncture, we have now elevated and evolved so we attract people and experiences that align with our new state of being.

This means happier customers and clients. Better interactions overall. It also inherently shows up as financial success. Happier customers and clients equal more sales and more engagement.

As we replace negative thought patterns around ourselves, we will find that our results will include better self-esteem, which equates to us making better choices for our health and wellness. We will also find that we will continue to make better choices within our relationships, adding boundaries and clarity in our choices.

In this state of being, we shift to receive. After showing up and doing the work around limiting beliefs, we are now in the space to receive. This is the result of all our hard work, processing, and shifting. Now we get the benefits, just like in a job, but it's now our livelihood. We become the epitome of all that we have strived to become. Money comes and goes, but alignment is the true essence of arriving. And, ironically, as we become more in alignment, our priorities often shift. Those things that were important before are now replaced with more soul-enriching goals.

When we "get it," that's when we "get it." We get all of the blessings and get all of the abundance of what really matters.

Having gone through the processes, shifting my beliefs, creating new neuropathways, my mission is to help others. We can only help others to the level that we have helped ourselves. It is from this grounded standpoint that I show up. When I can help others through their own process, guide them in shifting their beliefs, and help them become more aligned.

I invite you to connect with me by email:

BookBonnieNow@gmail.com or www.BonnieSilver.com, and I will send you a FREE copy of "The B Guidebook - 7 Steps to BE'ing You."

About the Author

Have you ever crossed paths with a complete stranger and instantly felt you have known them all along?

Or walked into a coffee shop and had a conversation that changed your day, your week or your life?

Have you ever been moved to tears of joy and gratitude by a beautiful sunset, a kind gesture, or a random person or thing showing up at just the right time?

These are the types of experiences that people have when they meet and work with Bonnie L Silver. She is modest and completely unattached to the fact that she has a profoundly positive impact on the people she comes in contact with and the fact that, with little effort, they are transformed into her obvious and contagious joy, intuition, generosity and loving spirit.

Bonnie's passion is to help people on this journey of life to connect to their authentic self and from that place of love, instead of fear. She helps people dismantle the blockages and allow healing so they can manifest their best lives.

Whether it's connecting with her books and articles or coaching, she knows that to build a better society, the transformation begins at home within oneself. Bonnie lives and breathes what she believes in. She shares from her own experience and wears the scars – but without the pain. Which is why she is qualified to do what she does – shining her light and making this world a better place for her being here.

Connect with Bonnie L Silver, Author, Speaker and Consultant

Founder of Silver B Resources, LLC www.SilverBresources.com

Facebook @ https://www.facebook.com/BonnieLynSilver

Linkedin @ https://www.linkedin.com/in/bonnielsilver/

Instagram@ https://www.instagram.com/bonnielsilver/

Chapter 2

Overcoming Fear of Failure During Times of Change

"Don't permit fear of failure to prevent effort."
– John Wooden

By Mark Guidi

A "geek" by training (computer science and systems engineering), I learned early on that unless the code or system designs were precisely correct, things would not work. Perfection was mandatory as there was no other path—it either worked or it didn't, black or white. In addition, when things do go wrong, it is often private (i.e., if code doesn't work when building or testing it, usually only the programmer knows while they continue to refine it).

Over the years, I carried that black-or-white, one-path-to-success mindset with me into business and life in general. However, I quickly learned that business and life exist in the grey, where there are often multiple paths to follow and each of them can result in success or failure. In addition, those paths, and the success or failure they bring, are usually public, on display for all to see. This divergence between my mindset and reality led to huge amounts of fear as I strove to avoid failure at all costs in an imperfect world.

Over time, I had to unlearn that perfectionist mindset, overcome the fear, and get comfortable with failure. It's a lesson I continue to learn and re-learn all the time, having had a few setbacks, one of which landed me in the emergency room with a suspected heart attack in my 40s (it was not, it turned out to be stress). However, to be successful in business, life, or any time of change, one of the pre-requisites is being comfortable with failure. This does not mean being OK with failure, but rather understanding it will happen, learning from it, and continuing to move forward without letting it bog you down. It goes without saying that unmanaged fear of failure can lead to severe mental, emotional, and physical consequences as well as paralysis, so nothing gets accomplished.

As it turns out, I have gone from my early days as a black or white computer programmer and systems designer to leading large and small organizations through large-scale change events. This has forced me to come to grips with failure and not fear it. What follows is what I learned about failure and some techniques I and others have used to manage the fear of failure.

Understanding Fear

Before you can manage fear, you need to understand it and where it comes from. It is one of the most primal instincts, going back to long before humans existed. Fear originates from a combination of biochemical reactions and the corresponding emotional response. Most everyone has heard of the classic "fight-or-flight response," where, based on a life-or-death situation, an animal will instinctually try to survive by either running ("flight") or, if that's not possible, fighting. While most of us don't face physical life-or-death situations every day, our brains are wired such that things that are not physically harmful, but rather emotionally or mentally stressful, can elicit the same response. For example, while no one has ever literally died from giving a poor public speech or having their project not yield the expected results, depending on the circumstance, you could get ridiculed, your career could be impacted, or your ego could be severely bruised. Some internalize this as a kind of death (e.g., embarrassment or career limiting), and fear of such an outcome elicits the same fight-or-flight response in the human body.

When considering times of personal or professional change specifically, fear is an instinctive emotional reaction to the unknown that change brings forth. For example, when a business is going through a transformation, staff worry they may lose their jobs if the company does not perform well, or that they could be replaced if their skills become outdated. This is especially true in the modern era with Artificial Intelligence (AI). Once that initial thought of concern enters the mind, it frequently cascades down the black hole of fear as you quickly imagine how either of these outcomes could jeopardize personal status and family financial stability. An example of a typical pattern is: the company's financials are not where management wants them to be; to reduce costs, they are looking to automate. This then gets internalized and personalized: I may not be able to keep up given my skill set; I will most likely lose my job; without a job, I can't pay bills; I will lose my house, my car, my family, everything ... and down the black hole of fear you go.

This kind of fear stems from the fact that change is seen as a loss of that which you know and feel comfortable with. Organizational psychologists have shown that when the status quo is perceived as threatened, this triggers fear that, in turn, may lead to defensive behaviors (Bridges, 2009).

At the personal level, fear is generated through the perception that change will overwhelm an individual's ability to adapt or upset customary, known rhythms. It could be something as simple as an office move, where a company relocates to a different part of town. Not really a big deal because, unlike a personal move, employees only need to show up at the new location. However, even this simple change can create stress through a fear of a new commute: Will I still have time to drop kids at school and get to work on time? What will traffic be like on the new drive? If I'm late, will I lose my job? etc.

Organizationally, or at a group level, fear can be a shared mindset that suppresses creativity, silences candor, and fosters resistance to useful change. In business, the job of managers and leaders is to be attuned to the early signs of fear and react to them purposefully and empathetically. This recognition and intervention are part of creating a space in which learning, development, and adaptation can occur. Coping with fear as a legitimate aspect of change enables leadership to develop and execute effective responses that direct fear as a resource as change occurs (Kotter, 1996).

Understanding Fear as a Change Leader

Chances of failure increase during times of change. Because many things are new and being tried for the first time, it is inevitable that some will not work out as planned. These "failures" can make or break a business change initiative depending on how they are handled. If they are handled as is typical, where the person leading the change effort is ridiculed or punished for the failure, it can dampen the organization's willingness to try new things, and the change effort will come to a screeching halt. On the other hand, if failures are seen as learning opportunities and the leader is allowed to try again, the organization will become more comfortable with failure and over time begin to try more new things. The key is to not make the same mistake twice.

This approach works with personal change as well. If you consider yourself the leader of change in your own life, getting comfortable with things not always working out is key. I'm reminded of a time when a close friend was determined to lose quite a bit of weight. She launched out on her personal change journey of diet and exercise, and was doing well. But then came some weddings and other events, and she ended up gaining a few pounds back and was so frustrated with herself. I remember talking to her about this and reminding her that while she could look upon this as a "failure" the key is to learn from it and move on, not to get hung up on the misstep. Change is never a straight path, so we spoke about what she could do differently next time to try and avoid that same "failure" (which I never viewed as a failure). One option would be to not go out anymore until she hits her weight target. However, that is more like giving in to your fear. An alternative is to embrace it and plan for missteps by perhaps allowing yourself one cheat per week, so you know it's coming. Whatever the approach, the key is to make it sustainable and fun. She did this and other things along the way and successfully lost over 30 pounds and kept it off. A huge victory.

Managing Fear as a Leader

As a change leader, before you can help others, much less an entire organization, get comfortable with their fear of failure, you must first master your own. As with many soft skills, this will come more easily for some than others, so if it takes you a while, that's OK. It starts by developing a positive mindset even in the face of adversity and challenge. This does not mean to be Pollyannaish, seeing only the positive and ignoring the challenges. Rather, it is about continuing to focus on the desired outcome and solving problems as they arise, always moving toward the end goal, even if not in a straight line. As many top-performing athletes have learned, skill and expertise get you to the game, but a positive mental attitude is how you win and become a champion.

While this all probably sounds obvious, putting it into daily practice is not easy and requires discipline. Here are five techniques you can employ to help stay positive and focused on the end goals while minimizing (not eliminating) the fear of failure.

1. **Don't take things personally**. Accept that failure will happen, and it's not a direct reflection on you or your worth. After all, change inherently means doing things differently than they have been done before and therefore are ripe for errors. Learn from them, embrace the learning, and move forward. Don't beat yourself up.

2. **Develop a strong support network**. To help with this, find like-minded individuals both inside and outside your organization or circle of friends. They can serve as mentors or sounding boards to bounce ideas off of, as well as help you

navigate the tougher times when you are feeling down or something has gone wrong and you're working through it.

3. **Find ways to de-stress**. This is good advice for anyone in any line of work or life in general, but it is particularly important for change leaders or those going through a professional or life change event. Examples could include taking up yoga or meditation, exercising each day, unplugging and doing some hobby completely unrelated to work, or simply spending quality time with family or friends. Most successful leaders incorporate many of these into their lives. However, remember to focus not just on the physical, but mental, emotional, and spiritual as well—balance is key. My personal choice was martial arts, which encompasses many of those elements simultaneously.

4. **Develop a growth mindset**. Don't get wrapped up in the details of what's going wrong. Again, this doesn't mean ignoring things not going well, but viewing them as challenges to be solved. Address the problem, then move forward. By not concentrating on the failure but rather viewing it as a learning opportunity, it can lower the amount of stress failure causes. One of my favorite quotes in this regard is from Thomas Edison, who famously said, "I have not failed. I've just found 10,000 ways that won't work."

5. **Visualize success**. Regularly envisioning positive outcomes can shift focus from potential failure to achieving desired goals. This technique boosts confidence and helps leaders stay motivated while keeping an eye on the end goal. A good way to do this is to literally put a visual up that you can look at every day.

Managing Organizational Fear

Considering fear is something that cannot be avoided during times of change, organizations, like leaders, need to learn how to overcome fear. Leaders can employ a variety of tools to help organizations effectively address organizational fear. Here are seven techniques to do that.

1. **Be honest.** Fear is best managed by transparency. It is imperative to have frequent communications, open forums, and honest conversations about what the transformation is determined to achieve, where we are in the journey, and what we face as challenges. Not only does it keep employees in the loop, but it also signals that management recognizes and respects their need to have a clear picture of the future. Scheduled town hall meetings, in-depth internal memos, and a separate intranet page for change updates can all demystify the process and let employees know that leadership is handling change transparently (Kotter, 1996). It's equally important to inform organizations when you don't know something. That avoids the fear generated by rumors that leadership is hiding something. If you don't know or a decision has not been made, say that, but also say by when you believe that information will be available, and then ensure it is, or at least follow up.

2. **Do it with them, not to them**. People are more receptive to change when they have a role or voice in how it is implemented. The best way to calm fears is to create avenues for input, whether in the form of workshops, focus groups, or just one-on-one meetings. Allowing group members to offer

their input can help them move from feeling like passive victims of change to active participants in change. Involvement breeds ownership, and when people feel their ideas and concerns are being thoughtfully considered, even if every idea is not acted upon, resistance falls away. It also enables leaders to get feedback about where the pitfalls might be occurring in the change process and take action to address them before they become a real problem (Bridges, 2009).

3. **Promote a culture of psychological safety.** Psychological Safety is defined as a shared belief held by members of a team that it is safe to take risks in the face of uncertainty. It is necessary to have this environment for walking the path of uncertainty, which is, in this case, the change event. Leaders can promote psychological safety by rewarding experimentation, fostering open conversations about failure, and letting mistakes serve as learning experiences rather than punishing them. It also sets the tone that it is OK to fail occasionally, which will help the rest of the organization embrace taking the kinds of risks necessary for successful change. According to studies by Edmondson (1999), teams working in psychologically safe work settings measure higher on key drivers of learning and innovation that are necessary in times of change.

4. **Provide training and new skills development.** Fear often stems from one's comfort level in being able to perform adequately in a new situation. This makes training and new skills development paramount to helping overcome organizational fear. Tailored training programs, mentorship

programs, and the forging of external partnerships with organizations focused on professional development can help make this transition easier. It's been shown that when organizational members feel they are competent and comfortable in their new role, they view change as an opportunity rather than a threat (Schein, 2010).

5. **Lead with calm and confidence.** Leaders set the tone in an organization, and this is even truer during times of change, when everything is more exaggerated. Emotions are contagious, and when a change leader demonstrates tranquility, self-assurance, and a positive outlook, these emotional signals can be infectious. Confident, measured behavior from the leadership team will assure the organization that the process of change is effectively managed. Conversely, a leader who is anxious, stressed, and emotional can have the opposite effect. Hence the need for change leaders to address their own anxieties and fears first, as previously discussed.

6. **Acknowledge wins and milestones.** An antidote to fear can be the rejoicing in and celebration of progress. "Those first wins, in the context of the enterprise transformation, act as proof of concept that change is taking place" (Kotter, 1996). Wins build stamina and give proof of concept that the organization is on the correct path. Celebrations vary in their manifestation from public to private forms and in their effect in boosting morale, but all are important in helping manage fear. This works in personal situations as well. Harkening back

to the weight loss example, once you lose that first 5 or 10 pounds, celebrate the milestone.

7. **Use coaching and peer support**. Lastly, consider utilizing external coaching and peer-based support structures. Coaching offers customized advice and support to individuals, whereas peer networks make available communities in which people can come together to talk through experiences, issues, and strategies as they experience change. Leaders who provide strong support systems are perceived as caring for their employees' welfare, which fosters trust and minimizes resistance (Edmondson, 1999).

Managing fear is a critical factor that determines the success of any change, personal or professional. Unmanaged fear, if not addressed, will result in poor performance, loss of willpower, and at the organizational level, a loss of talent or, at a minimum, a greater resistance to change. In contrast, when fear is properly managed through transparent communication, involvement, targeted training, and psychological safety, the foundation is laid for a more resilient and innovative workforce or individual. Learn to embrace fear, learn from it, and have fun!

References

1. Bridges, W. (2009). *Managing transitions: Making the most of change.* Da Capo Press.

2. Edmondson, A. C. (1999). Psychological safety and learning behavior in work teams. *Administrative Science Quarterly, 44*(2), 350–383. https://doi.org/10.2307/2666999

3. Kotter, J. P. (1996). *Leading change.* Harvard Business Review Press.

4. Schein, E. H. (2010). *Organizational culture and leadership* (4th ed.). Jossey-Bass.

Suggestion for Further Reading

1. Jeffers, S. (2007). *Feel the fear and do it anyway.* Vermilion

About the Author

Mark A. Guidi's introduction to transformational leadership began with a misstep in a high-profile transformation early in his career which taught Mark a profound truth: leading change is fundamentally different from leading traditional operations. Since then, he has led transformational programs spanning Fortune 500 companies, private equity owned firms, and nonprofits. He has discovered that meaningful change occurs not through force but via clarity, agility, and a human-centered perspective.

Mark serves as a trusted advisor and a leader of growth, guiding teams through acquisition integrations, carveouts, operational restructurings, and billion-dollar pivots. His approach has yielded remarkable results:

- 5X revenue growth and a 10-point EBITDA increase at a PE owned firm through the integration of six companies in four years.

- 8X improvement in member experience and winning national awards for the first time in organization's century plus history for a national non-profit organization.

- $2B in unlocked annual revenue through a three-year, billion-dollar investment.

Beyond the metrics Mark's leadership is grounded in systems thinking, martial arts discipline from decades of training, and a global perspective shaped by years living and working across Asia and Europe. Mark holds an undergraduate degree in computer science and graduate degrees in systems engineering and organizational design as well as certifications in executive coaching and AI business strategies. This allows him to blend technical acuity with human insight to achieve successful outcomes.

Today, he continues to lead transformation and growth initiatives as well as writing and coaching to help others navigate change and achieve the growth they want with courage, clarity, and purpose. If you are looking to undertake a major transformation or life changing event, follow Mark on LinkedIn or reach out to him at mark@markguidi.com.

Chapter 3

It Was Never Failure, It Was Fear

By Shree Rego

I've launched companies, from an event management business to a charming cupcake store I built from scratch during a recession. On the outside, each one looked like a bold leap of entrepreneurship. And they were. But what I've come to understand over the years is that the biggest leap I ever took wasn't the business idea, it was daring to believe in myself long enough to see it through. What eventually unraveled those dreams wasn't a lack of passion, creativity, or effort. It was something subtler and far more powerful: my own thoughts. The fear, the self-doubt, the limiting beliefs that crept in quietly and sabotaged the very success I worked so hard to build. No one teaches you that in business school. No one tells you that the real CEO of your business is your mindset.

What They Don't Teach in School

They teach us math, English, history, science, physical education, and how to pass a test. We learn about supply and demand, a bit of marketing, and maybe some leadership strategies. And while all of that has value, what they don't teach us is that our beliefs are what truly make or break our business, and our lives. They don't teach us that our thoughts carry energy, and that energy has power.

No one ever pulled me aside and said, "Hey, just so you know, if you don't believe you're worthy of success, it won't matter how good your idea is." Or that the subconscious fear of failure can quietly erode every win before it even happens. If only I had known sooner. But that would not have permitted the lessons (and learning from failure) that contributed to my current success in my mindset, personal life, and business.

I've learned that success is never just about hard work; it's about inner work. The things we don't see but feel: the fear of being seen, the belief that we're too much or not enough, the weight of proving ourselves. I had all of it running in the background, unconsciously shaping every decision I made.

I've come to understand that our minds are the true starting place of every venture. That our thoughts shape our vibration, and that vibration affects our actions, and those actions determine whether we rise or retreat. Years ago, I didn't know how to rewire my limiting beliefs, or frankly, what that even meant. I didn't know how to regulate my nervous system during high-stress moments, or how to recognize self-sabotage disguised as playing it safe. I reacted instead of responding. I resisted instead of receiving.

The reality is, until we "sit with our sh*t" as I teach to my clients, and understand our own inner conflict—often rooted in fear and hidden under layers of perfectionism, overworking, and imposter syndrome —it will eventually catch up with us. No amount of external success will ever be sustainable if your internal world is shaky.

Once I began understanding the neuroscience behind mindset, how thoughts become patterns, and patterns become results, it changed how I approached things. Pairing that with what I now see as a spiritual truth, that our energy attracts our outcomes, became the foundation of my personal evolution. But back then, I didn't have those tools. I had drive, talent, and passion, but my thoughts still ran the show. And during one of the most inspired business ventures of my life, those thoughts nearly took it all down.

The Cupcake Store: A Miracle in the Making

My cupcake shop was magic. I had zero prior experience in food retail, but I had a vision, and more importantly, I had fire. I believed in the brand, the product, and the experience I was creating. I hustled. I handcrafted the concept from scratch. I designed the shop to feel warm and inviting, a little boutique serving over 25 flavors of specially designed cupcakes daily. We specialized in designing logos on each cupcake as well as beautiful wedding cupcake towers and cakes. I learned everything I could about creating recipes, sourcing, branding, and customer service. And for a while, it worked. Business was good. People lined up waiting for their cupcake orders. Local buzz started growing. It felt like I had created something truly special from nothing. Heck, I was even on local television shows several times, and my beautifully designed cupcake box was seen on the show Wife Swap! Proud couldn't begin to describe my emotions at the time.

Then, halfway through, the recession hit. It was 2008.

The economy crashed. I started to panic. In addition, the town that my lovely shop was located in was undergoing a sidewalk and street construction upgrade, making it challenging for the local stores to receive customers because walking and parking were a nightmare. But here's the truth I didn't see at the time: It wasn't the recession that ultimately unraveled the business. It was me. My *thoughts* started to shift before my numbers did. I began to question myself. *Who am I to think I could pull this off? What if this was a fluke? Maybe I'm not cut out for this after all.*

I started shrinking, second-guessing every decision, and playing smaller, trying to hold it all together instead of innovating and believing forward. The stress caused my fear to escalate to a point where my creativity was slowly vanishing. My problem-solving was fueled by fear. I now see how my own fear—triggered by circumstances, yes, but fed by old stories of unworthiness—began to seep into everything. Into my leadership, into my energy, into the business itself.

And still, when I look back, I am wildly proud of what I built. The cupcake store was a miracle. It was bold. It was beautiful. It was proof that I could take a dream and make it real. The failure? That wasn't a reflection of my abilities; it was a reflection of the beliefs I hadn't yet learned how to transform.

Now I know better. Now I teach others that mindset isn't a side note in entrepreneurship, it's the core. It's the *real* foundation. Because no matter how solid your business is, if your inner narrative is shaky, everything else eventually follows.

The Event Company: Juggling Success and Survival

Before the cupcake shop, I launched an event management and catering company. I loved it, bringing visions to life, curating experiences, watching people gather, celebrate, and connect. It was a fast-paced, creative business that lit me up. Clients were happy, referrals were coming in, and on the outside, it looked like I had everything under control.

But behind the scenes, my personal life was unraveling.

I was in a toxic and emotionally abusive marriage. I was pregnant. And I was doing everything I could to keep my business afloat while holding together a private world that felt like it was breaking me apart. The pressure was immense. I started losing focus, not because I didn't care, but because I was fighting invisible battles that no one else could see.

Eventually, the stress and emotional strain took over. I was physically showing up, but mentally and emotionally drained. The business that once brought me joy started to feel like a burden, not because it wasn't working, but because I wasn't. I didn't yet know how to regulate my emotions, create boundaries, or believe that I deserved peace and success at the same time. Once again, the root of what went wrong wasn't logistics. It was the unhealed, unchallenged beliefs I carried: that I had to prove my worth through overworking, that I couldn't have both happiness and success, that I had to suffer to earn.

Looking back now, I don't carry shame, I carry pride. I built that business with passion and creativity. But I also recognize how my inner world dictated my outer results. That business taught me more about survival, resilience, and the cost of silence than any course ever could.

From Fearful Thought to Empowered Action

Eventually, I started waking up to the truth: It wasn't bad luck or poor timing that caused my patterns; it was my thoughts.

So, I got to work.

I became obsessed with understanding how the mind works, why we self-sabotage, and why fear feels so real even when our dreams are within reach. I studied mindset rewiring, past trauma healing, neuroplasticity, spiritual law, and energy work. I stopped just "doing" and started *becoming* the kind of woman, leader, and business owner who could recognize fear and still move forward anyway.

I started catching myself in the act of shrinking. I became aware of the way doubt would creep in disguised as caution. I created rituals to shift my energy, through affirmations, visualization, breathwork, and micro goal setting. I learned to recognize when self-sabotage was trying to creep in and why. I learned how to parent my inner voice and "sit with my sh*t" to recognize what inner thoughts were contributing to the fear that would ultimately continue to hold me back.

I didn't achieve this overnight. It was years of working from the inside out. But once I did, with consistent steps and discipline, I felt the shift, the change. Not just in business, but in life. I stopped building from fear and started building from belief. I stopped needing external success to prove my worth and started embodying the truth that I'm worthy because I exist—and so are you!

Create Anyway

If you have an idea tugging at your soul, don't wait, *create it*. If you're waiting for the fear to go away before you leap, it most likely won't. So, leap anyway. Because fear doesn't disappear by waiting. It dissolves through movement. It softens through proof. It fades as you take one step, then another, retraining your mind to trust your inner wisdom instead of the noise of doubt. You don't need to have it all figured out; you just need to begin. Begin messy if you need to.

What I've learned through building, failing, and rebuilding businesses is this: The most powerful strategy in the world means nothing if your thoughts are rooted in lack. But if you nurture your inner world, if you believe with conviction, align with your deepest intention, and choose courage over comfort, you become unstoppable.

Failure didn't ruin me. It refined me. It cracked me open, shed my ego (always a work in progress), and revealed my ability to keep trying. It prepared me for bigger visions and deeper alignment. It strengthened my fear muscles and reminded me that I can get back up every single time. That the future outcome is never as dire as my fearful thoughts lead me to believe.

Fear didn't disqualify me. It became my compass once I learned to face it head-on. Every time I faced fear, it was pointing me to my next level of growth.

And your thoughts? They can either be your loudest critic or your greatest ally. You get to choose.

You don't have to be fearless to be successful. You just have to stop letting fear drive your decisions. Every time you choose belief over doubt, action over avoidance, and faith in your vision over the inner noise, you elevate. You empower yourself. You become the kind of entrepreneur who doesn't just build businesses, but builds a *legacy*, one rooted in courage, self-trust, and your own personal power.

If I've learned anything on this journey, it's that success doesn't begin with funding, strategy, or perfect timing. It starts in the mind and with the way you speak to yourself. With the mirror. With the moment you stop waiting... and decide to *create anyway*.

Because the truth is, your outer world will always mirror your inner world. You can have the best idea, the most impressive credentials, or the perfect branding, but if you don't believe in yourself at the core, it's like building a dream on quicksand. That belief doesn't come from reading one motivational quote or watching a TED Talk. It comes from doing the deeper work, the sometimes messy, uncomfortable, raw work of unlearning who you thought you had to be and remembering who you truly are. This is the work so few choose to do and find themselves repeating patterns that do not serve them.

That's what I guide my clients through today. We don't just talk strategy, we heal, we rewire, and we get radically honest. We explore the fears behind the procrastination, the perfectionism behind the burnout, the self-doubt behind the silence. Because that's the real work. That's where transformation lives.

I'm not here to pretend it's easy, but I am living proof that it's possible. That you can rise from fear. That you can create a life and business that feels aligned with your soul. That every setback is a setup for a comeback if you choose to see it that way.

So, if you're in the middle of a transformation, a breakdown, or even a breakthrough, know this: The moment you start believing that your inner healing is just as important as your outer hustle, everything begins to shift. That's where your true power lives. And it's yours to claim.

About the Author

Shree Rego is a deeply intuitive, purpose-led coach, entrepreneur, speaker, and retreat leader who blends spiritual wisdom with grounded, transformative action. Her work centers around intention setting, mindset rewiring, and helping individuals break free from fear and doubt so they can step into clarity, confidence, and empowered action. Shree believes that true transformation begins by understanding and shifting the patterns and beliefs that hold us back.

With deep empathy rooted in her own healing journey, Shree specializes in guiding women who are recovering from toxic and abusive relationships. Her global coaching and retreat business is built on the belief that healing and growth require courageous inner work— and that through this work, we reclaim our power and rewrite our story.

Before entering the corporate world as a Vice President in residential property management, Shree owned and operated multiple businesses, blending entrepreneurial experience with intuitive insight. After building a successful corporate career, she chose to return to her entrepreneurial roots, driven by a calling to help other women heal, grow, and step fully into their potential.

As a sought-after speaker, Shree is known for her raw honesty, powerful presence, and ability to deeply connect with her audience. Through one-on-one mentorship, immersive retreats and workshops, and live speaking engagements, she helps others break through limiting beliefs, fear, and self-sabotage—so they can finally live in alignment with their truth and purpose.

The best way to connect with Shree is through her website at ShreeRego.com, on social media @shreeregocoaching, or on LinkedIn @ShreeRego.

Chapter 4

What Is 'Real' Anymore?

By Dr. Brian Grossman

In an age where filters mask flaws and algorithms shape attention, the first act of rebellion is remembering what's real.

Introduction: The Age of Artificial Everything

Last Tuesday, I watched my eight-year-old nephew discover that his favorite YouTube creator wasn't actually a kid like him, but a sophisticated AI avatar. The disappointment in his eyes was profound—not just because he'd been deceived, but because he suddenly questioned everything he'd believed about his digital heroes. His emotional response was immediate and visceral: betrayal, confusion, and a kind of existential vertigo that made him ask, "How do I know what's real anymore?"

In that moment, I recognized something I'd been studying for years—the collapse of what psychologist Jean Twenge calls our "reality anchors." My nephew's generation, what Twenge terms iGen or Gen Z, has never known a world without smartphones, social media, or algorithmic curation. For them, reality isn't something discovered through direct experience—it's something delivered through screens, shaped by artificial intelligence, and constantly shifting based on engagement metrics.

In contrast, I remember a moment from that same week: sitting with my grandfather on his porch, no phones in sight, listening to him tell stories about his childhood. His weathered hands gestured as he spoke, his voice carried the weight of lived experience, and in that analog moment, everything felt unfiltered and real. The difference was striking—one experience left me questioning truth itself, while the other anchored me in it.

This brings us to a provocative question that defines our era: When was the last time you felt truly yourself, unedited and unobserved? More importantly, how does living in an artificial reality affect your emotional well-being, your relationships, and your sense of purpose?

The Collapse of Certainty

There was a time when truth felt solid—rooted in shared experience, community, and evidence. Our great-grandparents gathered around radios for news, trusting Walter Cronkite's voice to deliver facts. Communities shared stories passed down through generations, creating collective meaning through ritual and repetition. Truth was verified through multiple sources, debated in town squares, and built on the foundation of shared values.

But today, we swim in a digital sea of interpretations, impressions, and illusions. From social media posts to AI-generated videos, reality is no longer what we see or hear—it's what the algorithm decides to show us. We've moved from a world of scarce information, where truth was precious and carefully curated, to one of infinite information, where truth is whatever captures our attention longest.

Jonathan Haidt calls this crisis an "epistemic collapse"—a breakdown in the systems by which we collectively discern truth. Jean Twenge adds that this new generation has never known a world without digital mediation of reality. Her research reveals that heavy social media use among teens correlates with rising rates of anxiety, depression, and what she calls "reality disconnection syndrome"—a feeling of living in a simulation rather than authentic life.

The psychological impact is profound. When we can't trust our perceptions, our emotional regulation systems become hypervigilant. We're constantly scanning for threats, validating our experiences through external metrics, and losing touch with our internal compass. This is what researchers call "digital dysregulation"—a state where our emotional responses are shaped more by artificial stimuli than authentic experiences.

Shifting Foundations of Reality: How Fast the Ground Shifted

Consider how rapidly our information landscape transformed, and notice the emotional milestones along the way:

1995: The World Wide Web goes mainstream. Information becomes democratized, but still requires effort to find. *Emotional tone: Curiosity and optimism.*

2004: Facebook launches. Social connection becomes digital, but still primarily connects real-world relationships. *Emotional tone: Excitement about connection.*

2007: The iPhone is released. The internet becomes portable, and constant connectivity begins. *Emotional tone: Convenience mixed with first hints of anxiety.*

2010: Instagram launches. Life becomes performative, filtered, and curated for public consumption. *Emotional tone: Comparison and inadequacy emerge.*

2016: TikTok arrives globally. Truth becomes whatever goes viral, regardless of accuracy. *Emotional tone: Addiction and shortened attention spans.*

2020: Deepfakes become accessible. Reality itself becomes malleable and questionable. *Emotional tone: Confusion and paranoia.*

2023: ChatGPT and AI tools explode. Human and artificial intelligence begin to blur indistinguishably. *Emotional tone: Existential uncertainty about human value.*

In less than three decades, we've gone from information scarcity to information chaos. We are, as Twenge warns, overstimulated but undernourished. Our minds aren't just infected with viruses of code—they're infected with viruses of belief, comparison, and artificial urgency.

Life in the Filtered Lane

Take Instagram: a gallery of "authentic" moments that are anything but. We see sunlit breakfasts, perfect relationships, travel snapshots—all filtered and framed to evoke envy. The paradox is striking: users crave authenticity, yet present idealized selves. This is what researchers call *curated authenticity*—a performance of the real that triggers what positive psychology calls our "saboteur" voices.

In the framework of Positive Intelligence, saboteurs are the negative thought patterns that undermine our well-being. The digital age has spawned entirely new categories of saboteurs.

The Comparison Self-Sabotage: "Everyone else has a better life than me." Fueled by social media's endless highlight reel, this voice drives anxiety and depression.

The Validation Self-Sabotage: "I'm only worth what my metrics say I'm worth." This voice ties self-esteem to likes, comments, and shares.

The FOMO (Fear of Missing Out) Sabotage: "I'm missing out on something important." This creates compulsive checking behaviors and chronic dissatisfaction.

The Perfectionist Sabotage: "I must curate the perfect online presence." This leads to performative living and disconnection from our authentic selves.

Consider Sarah, a 28-year-old marketing professional I interviewed. She spent hours each Sunday planning her week's social media content, carefully staging "candid" moments, writing captions that seemed spontaneous but were actually workshopped with friends. "I felt like I was living my life twice," she told me. "Once for real, and once for the camera. Eventually, I couldn't tell which version was actually me."

The emotional cost was severe. Sarah reported feeling anxious when she couldn't post, depressed when posts didn't perform well, and increasingly disconnected from her actual experiences. Her saboteur voices had become louder than her authentic self.

Synthetic Personas and the Authenticity Crisis

This confusion isn't limited to social media. Deepfakes—AI-generated videos that convincingly mimic real people—further erode trust and trigger deep emotional insecurity. A politician's speech? A celebrity endorsement? A heartfelt apology? Any of these can now be manufactured with frightening accuracy.

In 2022, a deepfake video of Ukraine's President Volodymyr Zelensky appeared to show him surrendering to Russian forces. Though quickly debunked, the video demonstrated how synthetic media could be weaponized to spread disinformation during critical moments. The emotional impact was immediate: confusion, fear, and a profound sense that nothing could be trusted.

The authenticity industry has grown into a billion-dollar ecosystem: AI chatbots feigning empathy, wellness apps selling mindfulness like a product, and dating profiles powered by machine learning. Companies now sell "artificial intimacy"—chatbots designed to be your best friend, therapeutic companion, or romantic partner.

Dr. Sherry Turkle's research at MIT reveals that people form genuine emotional attachments to these artificial entities, often preferring them to human relationships because they're more predictable and less emotionally demanding. This creates what she calls "emotional outsourcing"—delegating our deepest human needs to artificial systems.

The Neuroscience of Artificial Reality

When we engage with artificial or curated content, our brains respond as if the experience were real. Mirror neurons fire when we watch others' experiences, even digital ones. Dopamine pathways activate when we receive social media validation, creating genuine addiction patterns.

Research by Dr. Anna Lembke at Stanford shows that digital stimulation triggers the same reward pathways as drugs, gambling, and other addictive substances. The constant stream of artificial experiences literally rewires our brains to crave more stimulation while finding real-world experiences less satisfying.

This creates what neuroscientists call "tolerance"—we need increasing amounts of digital stimulation to feel normal. Real conversations feel boring. Quiet moments feel uncomfortable. Authentic emotions feel too slow and complex compared to the quick hits of digital validation.

Who Are You, Really? The Identity Fragmentation Crisis

If identity can be edited, marketed, and sold, what's left of the real you?

Your digital self is not your full self. It's a projection that's filtered, fragmented, and often reactive. And the longer we inhabit those projections, the more disconnected we become from our deeper selves. We begin to mistake our online personas for our true identity, losing touch with our unfiltered thoughts, emotions, and experiences.

Twenge's research reveals that heavy social media use among teens correlates with rising rates of anxiety, depression, and loneliness. The more we consume artificial experiences, the more we feel unanchored in our own lives. Gen Z participants in her studies describe feeling like they're "living in a simulation" or "watching their lives from the outside."

One 19-year-old college student, Alex, told me: "I realized I was spending more time thinking about how to present my experiences than actually experiencing them. I'd be at a concert, but instead of losing myself in the music, I'd be calculating the best angle for my Instagram story. I wasn't living my life; I was producing it."

This identity fragmentation extends beyond social media. We create different versions of ourselves for different platforms: the professional LinkedIn self, the casual Instagram self, the anonymous Reddit self. Each platform rewards different aspects of our personality, encouraging us to fragment our identity across multiple digital spaces.

The result is what psychologists call "identity diffusion"—a state where we lose touch with our core self because we've spread our identity across so many artificial contexts.

The Emotional Toll: Recognizing Digital Dysregulation (Deception)

Living in artificial reality isn't just confusing—it's emotionally exhausting. Common symptoms of digital dysregulation include:

Emotional Symptoms

- Anxiety when separated from devices
- Depression after social media use
- Irritability when connectivity is poor
- Emptiness after digital binges
- Comparison-driven inadequacy

Physical Symptoms

- Phantom vibrations from phones
- Sleep disruption from blue light
- Tension headaches from screen time
- Restlessness without stimulation
- Fatigue despite constant entertainment

Cognitive Symptoms

- Difficulty concentrating offline
- Shortened attention spans
- Confusion about personal values
- Difficulty making decisions without external validation
- Memory problems due to external storage of information

Relational Symptoms

- Preference for digital over face-to-face interaction

- Difficulty with emotional intimacy

- Impatience with slow-paced conversations

- Decreased empathy for others' experiences

- Loneliness despite constant connection

The Realness Audit: Examining Your Authentic Self

Take a moment to reflect on these questions. Notice your emotional responses as you consider each one:

Identity Mapping

- Which parts of your online presence feel most authentic to who you are offline?

- What aspects of your personality do you hide or minimize in digital spaces?

- How do you behave differently when you know you're being observed or recorded?

- What emotions arise when you imagine losing all your digital personas?

Values Assessment

- What do you deeply care about that you rarely share online?

- How do your digital choices align with your stated values?

- What would you do differently if no one was watching or judging?

- Which of your online activities make you feel proud versus ashamed?

Relational Quality

- When did you last have a meaningful conversation without documenting it?

- How do your online relationships compare to your offline connections?

- What would you miss most if all digital platforms disappeared tomorrow?

- How often do you feel genuinely seen and understood by others?

Emotional Regulation

- How does your mood change after using different digital platforms?

- What triggers your strongest emotional reactions online?

- How often do you feel authentic emotions versus performed emotions?

- What helps you feel most centered and present?

The Human App: Your Internal Operating System

The Human App is not a piece of software. It's a metaphor for your inner operating system—your beliefs, values, boundaries, and sense of self. Just as we regularly update our phones and computers, we must intentionally update our internal systems to navigate this artificial world while maintaining our humanity.

Unlike the algorithms that govern our digital experiences, the Human App is designed to serve your growth, not exploit your weaknesses. It's built on five core pillars.

Self-Awareness: Understanding your authentic thoughts, emotions, and motivations beyond external validation.

Boundaries: Protecting your mental and emotional space from digital overwhelm and manipulation.

Values: Anchoring your decisions in what truly matters to you, not what trends online.

Emotional Mastery: Developing the capacity to feel and process emotions without immediately sharing or performing them.

Purpose: Connecting with meaning that transcends digital metrics and social approval.

The Human App operates from what Positive Intelligence calls the "Sage" perspective—the wise, calm, and creative part of your mind that can navigate challenges without being hijacked by saboteur voices.

The Enhanced Reality Check-In: A Daily Practice

Rebuilding your Human App begins with a daily practice I call the "Enhanced Reality Check-In." Each morning, before touching any device, spend five minutes with these questions:

Physical Awareness

- How does my body feel right now?

- What sensations am I experiencing?

- Where do I feel tension or relaxation?

Emotional Awareness

- What emotions are present for me right now?

- What saboteur voices might be active this morning?

- What would my Sage self be curious about today?

Relational Awareness

- What kind of human connection am I craving?

- How do I want to show up in my relationships today?

- What would it look like to be genuinely present with others?

Purpose Awareness

- What matters most to me today?

- How can I align my actions with my deepest values?

- What would I do if no one would ever know about it?

This simple practice helps you reconnect with your unfiltered self before the digital world begins shaping your attention and responses. It's a form of emotional inoculation, building your internal strength before encountering artificial stimulation.

Action Steps: Reclaiming the Real

The path back to authenticity requires intentional action that addresses both practical and emotional dimensions:

1. Create Sacred Analog Spaces

- Designate your bedroom as a phone-free zone.

- Keep a physical journal for unfiltered thoughts.

- Create a morning routine that doesn't involve screens.

- Practice one analog hobby that brings you joy.

2. Develop Emotional Regulation Skills

- Practice the "STOP" technique when feeling triggered online: Stop, Take a breath, Observe your emotions, Proceed with intention.

- Use breathing exercises to reset your nervous system after digital overwhelm.

- Develop a vocabulary for describing your emotions beyond "good" or "bad."

- Practice self-compassion when you notice saboteur voices.

3. Curate Your Digital Environment Consciously

- Unfollow accounts that consistently trigger comparison or negativity.

- Follow people who share vulnerabilities, growth, and genuine insights.

- Use apps that promote well-being rather than addiction.

- Set specific times for checking social media rather than constant scrolling.

4. Build Real-World Connections

- Commit to one substantive, phone-free conversation daily.

- Join activities that require face-to-face interaction.

- Practice being fully present with others without documenting the experience.

- Share something vulnerable with a trusted friend weekly.

5. Develop Critical Thinking Skills

- Question the source and motivation behind digital content.

- Fact-check claims before sharing them.

- Seek out diverse perspectives on important issues.

- Practice saying "I don't know" when you genuinely don't.

6. Strengthen Your Sage Voice

- Practice meditation or mindfulness to quiet mental chatter.

- Spend time in nature without devices.

- Engage in creative activities that don't require external validation.

- Read books that challenge your thinking and expand your perspective.

The First Act of Rebellion: Choosing Reality Over Simulation

In a world designed to confuse, *clarity is courage*. The systems profiting from your attention don't want you to pause, reflect, or question. They want you to be reactive, insecure, and constantly consuming.

But here's the revolutionary truth: You have more power than you realize. Every time you choose to pause before reacting, you're exercising your Human App. Every time you prioritize face-to-face connection over digital validation, you're strengthening your Sage voice. Every time you question whether something is real or artificial, you're practicing the essential skill of our age.

The first act of rebellion isn't dramatic—it's profoundly simple. It's the courage to sit quietly with your own thoughts. It's the wisdom to feel your emotions without immediately sharing them. It's the strength to value your authentic experience over your curated image.

The Daily Rebellion Checklist:

- I started my day without immediately checking my phone.

- I had at least one genuine, undocumented conversation.

- I questioned the authenticity of something I encountered online.

- I chose presence over performance in at least one moment.

- I felt and processed an emotion without immediately sharing it.

- I engaged with content that challenged my assumptions.

- I practiced self-compassion when I noticed saboteur voices.

The Journey Ahead

The path to emotional mastery in an artificial world isn't about rejecting technology—it's about relating to it more consciously. It's about developing the internal strength to navigate digital spaces without losing yourself in them. It's about building your Human App so robustly that you can engage with artificial intelligence while maintaining your human wisdom.

This journey requires what psychologists call "emotional courage"—the willingness to feel your authentic emotions even when they're uncomfortable, to sit with uncertainty even when quick answers are available, and to choose depth over speed even when the world rewards efficiency.

The stakes couldn't be higher. We're not just choosing between different ways of consuming information—we're choosing between different ways of being human. The question isn't whether artificial intelligence will change the world. The question is whether we'll maintain our humanity in the process.

So here's the challenge: Pause. Ask yourself—what parts of your identity are real, and what parts have been installed without your permission? The journey of this book is your reboot. It's a call to embrace your human complexity, your fallibility, and your truth, even when it doesn't trend.

The first act of rebellion is remembering what's real. Will you take it?

Chapter 5

Balancing Data Analytics With Intuitive Wisdom for Optimum Results

By Roben Graziadei, MA

> *Intuition is a very powerful thing.*
> *More powerful than knowledge.*
> *–Steve Jobs*

Steve Jobs, a father of technology and data advancement, valued his intuition over knowledge. In fact, regarding product development, after considering the data analytics, it has been said that he made his final decisions about which products to develop based on his intuition.

> *Intuition is the highest form of intelligence.*
> *–Albert Einstein.*

Albert Einstein, a genius physicist, saw intuition as paramount to his scientific data and discoveries, noting it as the highest form of intelligence.

Introduction

For 30+ years, I have been an advocate for my coaching clients to balance the use of data analytics with the wisdom of intuition, yielding optimum results. What does this look like? Why am I an enthusiastic advocate for my clients to make this approach part of their business acumen and strategic planning?

For answers to these questions, I share two examples. A CEO of a Fortune 500 tech firm in Silicon Valley, which I will unpack for you later in this chapter. The other is a restaurateur entrepreneur, which I will address in this introduction. For now, I will share a personal story of what balancing data analytics with intuitive wisdom looks like, where I first learned how to do this, and why it became my passion to teach it to others.

As a teenage girl, my dad, an airline captain and flight instructor, taught me to pilot a single-engine airplane. First, the training involved learning how to read the instruments and the data they provided to stay on course. If a pilot is slightly off course, they will arrive at the wrong destination. Also, the data provided by the instruments is for safety purposes. Herein lies mastering flight planning and using data from the cockpit instruments to navigate well.

Secondly, I was taught how to fly without instruments. Feeling the drag of the airplane and intuitively navigating safely and staying on course. When my dad told me that he was covering the instrument panel, my heart skipped a beat. He said, "Calm yourself, Roben. Lean into your intuition and feel the plane. You've got this!" I took a breath and relaxed into my deep inner knower. Holding the plane as steady as I could. Hopefully, staying on course and level with the horizon. I had no clue if I was on course and aligned with the horizon. I simply trusted my intuitive senses. Moments later, when my dad removed the flight panel covers, he said with glee, "Look, Roben, look"! Afraid of what I might see, I looked at the cockpit instruments. With absolute stunning amazement, the airplane was 100% on course and 100% level with the horizon. Never will I forget how that felt. It was both exhilarating and calming at the same time. That day, I learned the value of balancing data analytics with intuitive wisdom. Thus, the committed resolve to teach it to others was ignited in me. Not simply for the measurable breakthrough results that my clients have seen, such as 30% sales revenue increases year over year, or stronger profit margins, or doubling employee/student retention. But also, for an improvement in the quality of life, as you will see in the upcoming story of a restaurant entrepreneur. Before sharing his story, let us look at why this balance of data analytics and intuitive wisdom is so important.

In today's climate, I assert that developing this balance as part of your leadership and business acumen is imperative. There is a joke that says, "95% of all statistics are made up". It is no laughing matter though. Sadly, we have seen companies and individuals taken down when they manipulated and falsified data for ill gain.

Early on in my career as a marketing research analyst for Foodmaker, Inc., my job was to research and make product recommendations to executive leadership based on my analytical findings. I could have twisted the numbers every which way from Sunday to make the case for my favorite products. Here, too, I utilized the data but also transparently inserted my honest, intuitive gut feeling regarding product recommendations. The result was the introduction of one of the first healthy fast food menu items, the Pita Pocket Supreme. This opened the company to a unique niche with new customers, driving new business revenues. To date, this is still a successful menu item for Foodmaker, Inc.

That said, today we are bombarded with false data and fake news. AI is nothing more than data initially input by a person. The AI algorithms grow faster than we can keep up with. None of us might be able to track back to the original data source for verification. As said in the early days of technology onset, "Garbage In, Garbage Out." This applies now more than ever.

I am not saying that data is bad. Nor am I saying emphatically that data cannot be trusted. I am simply advocating that, based on these challenges leaders face, incorporating your intuitive wisdom as a data point is critical. I can tell you this. In my years of coaching clients, no one has ever expressed regret for listening to their intuition. However, many have expressed regrets for not listening to their intuition in decision making and for strategic planning. This is why I coach my clients to develop this balance as part of their leadership and business acumen. Take, for example, an entrepreneurial restaurateur client.

This restaurant owner hired me to help him identify continuous operational improvement opportunities for stronger profit margins and ways to drive new business sales revenue. As we holistically dissected his business, details of which are confidential and not to be shared here, we discovered operational areas for improvement, employee engagement approaches, and enhancements to sales and marketing. I asked him to take all the data and all the system analytics and sit with it for a few days. I taught him how to tune into and listen to his intuitive wisdom. He came back and said, "Here is what the data tells me. Also, here is what my intuition tells me." The net of it is that he streamlined operations, addressed some much-needed organizational issues, and, by trusting his gut, decided to hire a head chef.

The results of his choices are an 8% year-over-year increase in sales, improved profit margins despite hiring the chef and rising costs, maintaining consistent 4.7-star customer reviews, and optimized employee engagement/retention.

Of most importance, according to him, his quality of life has significantly improved. He has gone from working nearly 24/7 to taking a few days a week off and has been freed up to take time for himself, his family, and his holistic well-being.

This addresses what balancing data analytics with intuitive wisdom looks like and why it is so important. Let us now look at how my Fortune 500 tech client achieved optimum results using five steps from my coaching practice.

Step One—Identify your Current State (Undesired Outcomes)

Step Two—Identify your Desired State (Desired Outcomes)

Step Three—Analyze the Data and Incorporate Your Intuition

Step Four—Write your Strategic Plan (Steps to Achieve Your Desired Outcomes)

Step Five—Lead With Conviction/Execute With Decisive Action

Step One—Identify your Current State (Undesired Outcomes)

Just as with the restaurant entrepreneur, for confidentiality reasons, this client's story will speak in general terms versus specifics. This client, whom I will call John (not his name), came to me with a daunting Q4 challenge. As the CEO, the board was proposing to him a Q4 strategy to drive a stronger profit margin that John did not agree with. Feeling pressured, John called me and said, "I need to talk. I have a challenge that I need to talk through with someone that I trust will keep my confidence and has my company's best interest at heart. Someone with no personal agenda." Naturally, I was honored that he would reach out. When we met, he shared this. The board wants stronger Q4 margins than we have delivered on in Q1 through Q3. Their proposal is that we lay off employees in Q4 and rehire them in Q1. I probed with questions for a better understanding. Did they want to let employees know that in Q1, they would be hired back? What was their motive? Was it for shareholders, leadership bonuses, or a potential stock split? John's answers were troubling to both of us.

We set into motion Step 1—What is the Current State of the business? What are the undesired outcomes?

While the business was profitable, it was also starting to experience high employee turnover, with the salesforce and sales dropping slightly. Overseas operations were struggling with production deadlines, resulting in poor fulfillment of orders and customer complaints. John was concerned that laying employees off, even with an intention to hire back in Q1, would cause these pain points to escalate, irreparably hurting employee morale and customer relations. I agreed with his risk assessment. The question was what to do now?

Step Two—Identify your Desired State (Desired Outcomes)

Probing further, I asked a plethora of questions to help him clarify his desired state and outcomes. We studied 5 years of historical data on the company's employee turnover, sales ups and downs, and production fulfillment. We studied data trends in the Silicon Valley market with well-known tech companies facing similar issues. I presented him with studies of how layoffs affect morale, sales, manufacturing production, a company's brand, and even customer loyalty. Based on this data, John very clearly stated that he wanted to increase employee retention, improve production efficiency, and drive sales with a motivational Q4 sales promotion. He wanted to meet the board's demands for higher profit margins, NOT by laying employees off, but rather by driving the highest Q4 sales the company had ever seen. John wanted a win-win solution as espoused in Steven Covey's *The 7 Habits of Highly Effective People*. With John adamant about his current and desired state, we progressed to step three.

Step Three—Analyze the Data and Incorporate Your Intuition

Having completed thorough data analysis, John, anticipating push back, was not ready to present his plan to the board. He knew he needed more than data to take this stand and convince the board. This is where I began to teach him how to incorporate intuitive wisdom as a data point. I asked him thought-provoking questions intended to help him have an AHA moment. Advocating for him to have a nirvana awakening whereby he knew that he knew he could create an enterprise-wide winning solution that the board would agree to.

John's intuition urged him to team with the Chief Sales Officer to create a Q4 sales promotion that would yield breakthrough results. Results to drive unprecedented sales, increase employee engagement, morale, and retention, and with the Chief Operations Officer's help, a chance to implement new production. With unshakeable internal resolve, John was ready to prepare and present the team's Q4 strategy to the board.

Of note here, a cybersecurity executive colleague tells me that he always listens to his intuition when studying data. Otherwise, he risks getting lost in analysis paralysis, thereby potentially missing the big picture and a great opportunity.

Step Four—Write your Strategic Plan

Poised to write the strategic plan with specific actions for the C-team to take to bridge from an undesired state to a desired state, we identified John's WIG. A WIG is a Wildly Important Goal as taught in the *4 Disciplines of Execution*. In the strategic plan, we included weekly and daily steps for teams to act on to achieve the Q4 WIG. As expected, the board pushed back. John reported to me that he stood confidently before the board, backed by data and his intuitive wisdom, without wavering. The board rendered their support for John's strategy. John announced the Q4 sales promo and overseas production improvements, along with employee bonuses, once these goals were achieved at a companywide conference.

Step Five – Lead With Conviction/Execute With Decisive Action

Over the years, I have seen many leaders move forward with strategies that included data analytics and intuitive wisdom with successful outcomes that surprised even them. To lead with conviction and execute with decisive action for such results, one must have an internal resolve. An unshakable conviction. This comes from balancing data analytics with intuitive wisdom.

John led with conviction and inspired an enterprise-wide shared vision. John achieved his desired outcomes and more. Q4 sales were up 30% year over year. A company survey showed an improvement in employee morale. Production implementations doubled order fulfillment. Additionally, this company earned the reputation of having the best work environment, which has engendered employee loyalty in the competitive Silicon Valley marketplace.

Conclusion

Not only can the restaurateur entrepreneur and John the Fortune 500 CEO achieve these results. So can you!

Rumi, a philosopher and poet, said, "Be silent. Meaning is lost when there are too many words."

Proverbs 17:27 (NLT) says, "A truly wise person uses few words. A person with understanding is even tempered."

I encourage you, when conducting data analysis, to include your intuitive wisdom as a data point. A careful analysis of data along with your gut brings an inner resolve for sound decision making, prudent strategic planning, and execution. How do you know you are there? What does it look and feel like?

There is no talking out of both sides of your mouth.

There is no apologizing for your conviction.

Your tone is calm, not loud.

Your spirit is humble, not proud.

Your posture is elegantly confident, not cocky.

You are internally certain in an uncertain world.

You are unshaken by external forces.

Internal noise is replaced with peaceful mindfulness.

You are enabled and empowered.

In honoring the memory of my dad, and his words to his daughter when teaching her to fly: "You've got this!"

About the Author

Roben Graziadei has served 30+ years as an Executive Coach. She has coached 10k+ Fortune 500 Leaders and 500k+ persons/teams resulting in combined client growth of $50M+.

Her client's success is based on a winning formula balancing data analytics with the wisdom of intuition which she learned in her youth when taught by her dad to pilot a plane. Early on in her career Roben fought her own limiting beliefs. This is when her passion for balancing data with intuition was re-ignited as she learned to share data with executives while having the courage to stand up for her intuitive promptings. This ushered in prosperity and professional success. Later in her career as a Senior Consultant her clients expressed that their greatest regrets and biggest mistakes were in denying their intuition. This impassioned her to advocate for her clients to balance data with intuition to achieve optimum results.

Roben has a Masters in Counseling Psychology graduating with distinctions. She holds a BS in Business with a minor in statistical analysis. She began her career as a Marketing Research Analyst for a fast-food company, Foodmaker, Inc. She then joined FranklinCovey in the SFO/Bay Area as a Senior Consultant, later becoming a top sales performer and a featured keynote speaker. Roben was a Principal in the Tom Peters Group Consulting firm in Silicon Valley. As the Sales Director for Kaplan, Inc., she led the team to $1M+ in sales for a new division while facing the market obstacles Covid brought. Roben was a top sales leader/producer for 20 years running. She is the CEO of Net Result$, LLC, an executive coaching firm.

Roben's clients report a 30%+ increase in sales year over year, up to 97% increase in employee and student retention, 87% customer renewal, consistent 4.7 customer reviews, and a 50% increase in profit margins over 3 years, resulting in a combined client growth of $50M+ utilizing her unique approach.

Additionally, Roben is the bestselling author of *Exploring Management Styles*; she created, trademarked and authored *Instinctology*; she is a Marquis Women of Influence, a favored podcast guest and has created multiple training publications for her clients.

Schedule a complimentary call at
https://www.linkedin.com/in/robengraziadei/

Chapter 6

Breakthrough Presence: Why Your Next Level Requires a Shift in How You Show Up

By Victor Bullara, Certified Master Coach

You've practiced the presentation five times. You know the material cold. But as you step up to speak, your heart races, your mouth goes dry, your hands tremble—and your mind suddenly blanks.

"What's happening to me?" you wonder.

What you're experiencing is *Glossophobia*—the fear of public speaking. It's more common than the fear of death, and it strikes even the most experienced leaders. But what if the real issue isn't fear of public speaking... but a deeper fear of *being seen*?

The Invisible Factor That Elevates Influence

In every boardroom, on every stage, and across every Zoom screen, one unspoken force quietly determines who rises, who earns trust, and who gets chosen. It's not always intelligence, talent, or even experience. More often, it's something less tangible—but far more decisive.

It's Executive Presence.

You've seen it: the leader who walks into a room and instantly commands attention. The speaker who says little, yet somehow holds the space. The entrepreneur who doesn't just pitch, but inspires.

This article is about what that "it" factor really is, why it matters more now than ever, and—most importantly—how you can build it. Not through performance, perfection, or pretending, but through alignment, energy, and intentional practice.

The Confidence Crisis: Why Success Often Triggers Self-Doubt

If you've ever questioned whether you truly belong at the table, you're not alone. A staggering **84% of entrepreneurs** report struggling with **Imposter Syndrome**—the persistent fear of being exposed as a fraud, **even in the face of proven success**.

"Who am I to be doing this?"

"What if they find out I'm not ready?"

"Do I really deserve this level of influence?"

Ironically, the more accomplished you become, the more that voice tends to show up because every next level demands a new identity— one you haven't fully stepped into yet.

Imposter Syndrome isn't a weakness. It's a natural byproduct of growth. But if unaddressed, it chips away at your confidence and keeps your full presence from showing up in the room.

That's where Executive Presence becomes the game-changer. You don't need to fake confidence. You need to **anchor it** through presence.

What Executive Presence Really Is (And Isn't)

Many people mistake Executive Presence for charisma, style, or polish, but it's none of those.

Executive Presence is how others experience your **confidence, clarity, and energy** in every interaction, both verbal and nonverbal. It's the ability to project credibility and authenticity, even when you're uncertain. It's the quiet power that makes people say:

"That's a leader I trust."

Presence isn't about having all the answers. It's about having **alignment** between what you say, how you say it, and how people feel in your presence. And it matters everywhere:

- In pitch meetings where investors decide whether to back you

- In team settings where alignment and trust are built

- In public forums where thought leadership is established

Executive Presence doesn't just get you in the room. It makes you **undeniable** once you're there.

The 5 Pillars of Executive Presence™

After two decades of coaching more than 350 high-performing leaders, from startup founders to senior executives, I developed a practical, repeatable framework to help leaders strengthen their presence.

These are the 5 Pillars of Executive Presence™:

1. Gravitas—Calm, Grounded Authority

Gravitas is what makes people lean in when you speak. It's conveyed not through force, but through **poise, clarity, and stillness**.

Traits include:

- Remaining composed under pressure

- Speaking with conviction and intention

- Using pauses and body language to create credibility

Leaders with Gravitas don't dominate the room. They center it.

2. Communication—Clear, Compelling Delivery

Your ability to deliver ideas with clarity and resonance defines how deeply you influence others.

Key traits:

- Intentional, succinct messaging

- Adapting language to meet the audience where they are

- Using structure and storytelling to engage and inspire

Great communication isn't about being the most articulate—it's about being **memorable**.

3. Visibility—Strategic Influence

Visibility is about showing up **where it counts** and doing so with purpose.

It looks like:

- Having a presence in rooms where decisions happen
- Publishing insights where your ideal clients or stakeholders gather
- Advocating confidently for yourself and your ideas

Visibility is not vanity. It's how leaders scale their impact.

4. Energetic Presence—Nonverbal Credibility

Before you say a word, your energy introduces you. People read your tone, body language, and vibe **instantly**.

Energetic Presence means:

- Aligning your inner state with your outer signals
- Using posture, breath, and tone to convey confidence
- Projecting trust and presence—whether quiet or animated

Energy doesn't lie. It speaks before you do.

5. Emotional Intelligence—Relational Mastery

In every high-stakes moment, your ability to read the emotional landscape is crucial.

This involves:

- Sensing the unspoken dynamics in a room
- Adapting your tone and message based on cues
- Creating safety, rapport, and resonance with diverse audiences

Emotional intelligence turns communication into **connection**, and here's the truth: *Each pillar is a skill, not a personality trait.* Every one of them is coachable.

Why Even Brilliant Entrepreneurs Struggle With Presence

Many of the founders, entrepreneurs, and executives I coach are exceptional at what they do. They build innovative products, lead fast-scaling teams, and hit impressive revenue milestones. And yet, they feel invisible.

Here's what I often see:

- **They lead with content, not connection.** They talk about the features of what they built, but not the *meaning* behind it.

- **They rely on competence alone.** They assume "being real" is enough. But Presence isn't about being performative—it's about being *intentional.*

- **They wait to feel ready.** Instead of stepping into visibility, they stay behind the scenes, believing Presence will "catch up" later.

But Presence doesn't magically appear at the next milestone. **It's what gets you to the next milestone.**

"Your presence is either opening doors or quietly closing them."

Three Common Presence Gaps (And What They Mean)

After reviewing hundreds of presence assessments, three patterns emerge most often:

- **Gravitas.** Many leaders rush through key points, overexplain, or default to deferential language—even when they have authority.

- **Energetic Presence.** They show up physically, but their energy says "uncertain," "nervous," or "not ready."

- **Emotional Intelligence.** They miss emotional cues, respond uniformly, and struggle to adjust their approach mid-conversation.

These aren't signs of brokenness. They're **growth opportunities**—and help to create a clear roadmap to your next level.

5 Steps to Help You Build Breakthrough Presence

You don't need more credentials, more scripts, or more bravado. You need to start showing up with **intention and alignment**. Here's how:

1. Set a Presence Intention

Before every meeting, keynote, or investor pitch, ask: *"How do I want them to experience me?"* That question alone can transform your presence from reactive to *purposeful.*

2. Develop Gravitas Through Stillness

- Practice pausing

- Record yourself speaking and notice pacing

- Lower your shoulders, breathe deeper, and speak slower

You'll be amazed at how powerful calm can feel.

3. Elevate Energetic Presence

- Check in with your body before you speak

- Adjust posture, breath, and tone to reflect your message

- Remember: People respond to the **energy** behind your words more than the words themselves

4. Increase Strategic Visibility

- Share thought leadership on platforms where your audience gathers

- Say "yes" to visibility—panels, interviews, podcasts—even before you feel "ready"

- Make your work visible in the rooms that matter

5. Refine Communication with Structure

Think in three parts:

Point → Story → Call to Action

Simple, repeatable frameworks create clarity *and* impact.

A Real-World Transformation

One of my clients—an exceptional leader with 19 years of high-performing results and multiple promotions—was passed over for partnership. When she finally asked why, the feedback came back vague:

"You're missing executive presence." No one could define what that meant.

When I observed her during presentations, I noticed the patterns:

- She rushed her delivery
- Her voice would rise at the end of every sentence, making statements sound like questions
- Her eyes darted across the room, and she hid behind slides instead of leading with connection

Once we focused on developing her **Gravitas, Energetic Presence, and Emotional Intelligence**, everything shifted. She slowed down, made eye contact, and spoke with intention. She **led the room**, rather than simply speaking in it. The result? She was promoted to **Partner**, and soon after, was invited to keynote industry events and lead larger, more strategic projects.

Same expertise. Same intelligence. New Presence. **Bigger results.**

Your Turn: Where Is Your Presence Costing You?

What if your next breakthrough wasn't about effort, but about **how you show up?**

To help leaders get clarity on their strongest and weakest pillars, I created a complimentary **5 Pillars of Executive Presence™ Assessment**. It takes just a few minutes to complete and gives you instant feedback.

👉 Take the Free Assessment: https://go5pillars.com/
(You'll find it halfway down the page.)

Your score will highlight:

- Your current strengths

- Where your presence might be unconsciously limiting your impact

- Specific areas to focus on for growth

The most successful leaders I work with aren't perfect. They're **intentional.**

Final Thought: Presence Is the Portal

Executive Presence isn't for the elite. It's not something you're born with—or without. It's a trainable skill. A practiced art. A strategic advantage. And more than anything, it's your **invitation to lead louder, clearer, and more fully.**

The changes you need to make aren't dramatic, just little tweaks to how you approach the world, informed by greater self-awareness. Yet these tweaks can have huge effects. The more deliberate you are about how you show up, the more strategic and effective you can be at keeping your strengths in check and avoiding deeper problems.

So, let me ask you: Are you ready to build the kind of presence that opens rooms, earns trust, and makes you unforgettable?

Let's get to work.

About the Author

Victor Bullara has 35 years' experience in the Coaching, Human Resources, and Leadership Assessment/Development fields. Vic's experience includes 19 years as an HR practice leader for Ernst & Young, McBer (now Korn Ferry) and Development Dimensions International (DDI). He has coached, developed and mentored more than 450 leaders at the director level and above including 28 VP's and six SVPs of a $35 billion company, eight CEO's of a variety of companies (see below for details) and has more than 3,000 hours of executive coaching and development experience. He is an ICF credentialed coach and a Certified Master Trainer (from DDI). In the 14 years prior to starting his own executive coaching, and leadership assessment/development firm, Vic's direct corporate experience included HNTB Inc., (Western Division HR Director) Wipro (VP Human Resources) and ZLand.com (Chief Human Resources Officer).

He is also a co-author of the #1 best-selling book *Cracking the Rich Code* which was endorsed by Tony Robbins who described the book saying "success is predictable if you know what determines it. This book offers some valuable entrepreneurial insights that will strengthen your life, your business and your effectiveness overall."

Major Initiatives and Project Results Include:

1. Documented a 9:1 return on investment after six months of coaching a senior leader for a $100 million manufacturer.

2. For PepsiCo, developed leadership competency models for directors and vice-presidents at the corporate office at Taco Bell and Frito Lay. Worked closely with incumbents and high potentials to develop and implement individualized, leadership development plans.

3. Was part of the leadership team at eCompanies/Evercore, **a $300 Million venture fund** and evaluated business plans for investment purposes. Companies represented $2 billion in transformational technologies (like Business.com, eToys, Boingo Wireless, LowerMybills.com, and Ring.com). Went on to coach 7 CEO's in an effort to successfully launch their companies.

4. Designed a comprehensive leadership development and operations management program for global web-based solutions provider, delivering the content to audiences on three continents.

Education and Certifications

Victor has a degree in Psychology and Organizational Behavior from UCLA and taught HR courses at UCLA and UC Irvine for six years. He is a certified Executive/Master Coach, an International Coach Federation (ICF) Credentialed Coach, and a *Certified Winslow Dynamics Consultant.* He also completed (with "Distinction") the *Inspiring Leadership through Emotional Intelligence* program through

Case Western Reserve University. He is a certified Master Trainer through Development Dimensions International which allows him to draw upon 350+ hours of leadership and employee development programs. He is an Executive Coach to Executive MBA students at UCLA's Anderson School of Business. He graduated from UCLA with a degree in Psychology and Organizational Behavior. He also taught leadership courses at UCLA and UC Irvine for 6 years.

Victor Bullara, Certified Master Coach
✉ Vic@5Pillars.com
https://www.linkedin.com/in/vicbullara/

Chapter 7

Leading Change Through Possibility, Purpose, and People

By Jen Robertson-Hatanaka

As a leader, the way you show up during times of uncertainty, transformation, or adversity shapes how your team experiences their journey. I learned this early in my career when I was just stepping into my very first leadership role as a shift supervisor. Back then, I believed the most important parts of my job were the tasks I was responsible for, unlocking the doors, knowing the safe codes, and setting the break schedule. These responsibilities carried weight, and I was proud to have them and be trusted to complete them. But I missed something crucial, what truly mattered to my team wasn't how I completed the logistics, although important, but their experience was driven more by who I was when I carried those responsibilities. It was in my tone of voice, how I handled stress, whether I listened and gave recognition, and whether I was someone they could rely on during uncertainty. What they valued wasn't "what" I did, but rather "how" I did it. A good shift for them meant feeling respected, being seen for their work, and supported as they built new capabilities, and yes, a break schedule will help enable that experience. That has stayed with me and has been true regardless of my level of leadership or those I have led. How you show up in service of the team you lead is the foundation of their work experience and what sets them up to achieve great things.

Fast forward to today, and I've spent 25 years leading in the retail, hospitality, and customer service sectors, building empowered teams and guiding change through large-scale organizations. My approach is rooted in change leadership principles I've developed over time, an approach where people are invited to co-create the future, are believed capable of making contributions, and guided by one aligned vision. It's the difference between managing tasks or workload and inspiring transformation with a one team mindset.

Embracing Change, The Only Constant

You've likely heard the phrase "the only constant is change." It's often attributed to the Greek philosopher Heraclitus, who observed that life is in a perpetual state of flux. Change is everywhere. It has always been and always will be. It is both internal and external, deliberate and unexpected, and each of us responds to it uniquely. Some may feel energized by the endless possibilities, while others feel exhausted by the unpredictability. Often, how you see or react to change is shaped by personal experiences, maybe based on a current change you're navigating, a milestone that altered your course, or perhaps your "origin story"—the first change you consciously remember navigating.

In my case, change has been ever-present, and in fact, I seek it as a way of continuous improvement. I've always viewed it as a doorway or as an opportunity to create something new, refine what already exists, and challenge myself to grow. But let me be clear, just because

I embrace change doesn't mean I find it easy. It is often messy and feels like a dance of progress and setbacks. Then on the other side, when you can pause and reflect, it is rewarding to see who you've become because of the change and embed the learnings you gained from the journey—bumps, twists, bruises, and all.

One of my defining experiences with change was as a kid. By the time I entered grade eight, I had attended nine different schools; you could say my family moved a lot. Each school brought a new experience. Some schools I loved, and some I don't even remember. There were times I was the exciting "new kid" others wanted to get to know, and other times I found solitude as I quietly observed recess from the monkey bars. I adapted easily and wasn't fazed by changing schools; however, my sisters had entirely different experiences. There were best friends and stuffed animals lost in the shuffle, and sometimes a move meant sharing a bedroom or newfound freedom having your own. We all experienced and tell stories to this day that are different, even though we went through the same moves, same schools, and same household together. This taught me the fundamental truth that we each navigate change in our own way. That insight is simple but powerful and has deeply informed how I lead, focusing on others' experiences.

I've learned to listen, to approach with curiosity, and to create space for others to share what they are navigating, thinking about, and processing. Change, at its heart, is not just a strategy or a metric or the priority du jour; it is personal for those closest to the change. And as leaders, acknowledging that human element is what helps us turn disruption, uncertainty into a platform for possibilities.

Change Management vs. Change Leadership

Let's unpack a distinction I find essential in any transformational journey: the difference between change management and change leadership.

Change management is the architecture of change; it is the systems, disciplines, and data-driven processes that support it. It's the science needed in establishing the case for change, forecasting outcomes, allocating resources, and creating accountability structures. It's vital. In fact, not using these disciplines would be irresponsible. Your team, customers, and clients deserve clarity, logic, and a thoughtful framework for navigating change.

But change management alone doesn't galvanize a team. Change leadership is the art of inspiring a new movement forward. It's the human side of leading change through holding a clear and compelling vision, communicating it with transparency and empathy, and guiding your team forward with belief and intention. Change leadership asks you to walk the journey with your people, not just direct it from above, and it means empowering others to participate fully and shape the path itself, not just to be the executor of your directives.

Let's focus on exploring strategies that unlock change leadership. Successful change leadership begins by anchoring your approach in three pillars:

1. Sharing the Vision

2. Transferring Ownership

3. Establishing Co-creation and Collaborative Forums

Sharing the Vision and Creating Buy-In

At the start of any significant change, you are responsible for being clear with your team on these questions: *What will success look like, and why should I believe in it?* To answer them, you must craft a clear and authentic leadership message. This isn't just about explaining what's happening, although that is important. It's about making a compelling case for "why."

- Identify the problems the change is addressing

- Paint a vivid picture of success using metrics and experiences

- Acknowledge expected challenges

- Express your personal belief in the change and journey

This last part is key because your team wants to know not just the business logic for the change but your emotional investment, too. Why does this matter to **you**? What excites or concerns you? What makes you believe this path is worth it?

Authenticity is non-negotiable because people can feel it when you truly believe. I love the saying "only the truth sounds like the truth." Essentially, you know it when you hear it. I often advise leaders to partner with a coach or mentor to refine their message. It's so important to bounce it off someone who will give you balanced feedback. You have to do your homework to be confident and clear, and above all, you must be real.

Think of your message as the beginning of a conversation, not a command. It's opening up the room, so be sure you create space for questions, dialogue, and reactions. The goal is to move from *your* vision to *our* vision as one aligned team, and that shift happens through discussion, storytelling, emotional connection, and having space so that each person can make it theirs; that's when it becomes ours.

Transferring Ownership Activity

Once the vision is shared, the next step is transferring ownership. After all, it is important that the people closest to the work help define how the change gets implemented. This creates deeper engagement, empowers the team, and ensures the plan is practical.

Here's an activity I use to support this transition. It can be done individually or in facilitated groups (which I recommend). Ideally, bring in a third-party facilitator (a coach or trusted ally) so that you, as the leader, can observe, listen with curiosity, and assess your team's readiness for execution and implementation.

Ownership Activity

Open up the activity by sharing the importance that everyone is purposeful and intentional with their role in leading, implementing, or executing the change. Also, make it clear that what has always been done won't necessarily be what gets the team where they want to go, and that everyone is empowered to set that course through choices on what is needed, what isn't needed, and what is already possessed that serves the vision. Provide your team with these prompts to start to formulate their thoughts.

- What must I hold on to that is in service of our vision? What is already working towards that vision?

- What must I let go of to make space for the change needed? What does not serve the vision?

- What new skills, approaches, or capabilities do I need to acquire in order to be successful?

Give time for heads-down reflection and notetaking, encouraging honest and thoughtful responses. If this is a virtual exercise, consider using a Miro board for your team to capture live notes.

Then, move into sharing and discussion. This is where the magic happens. People grow confidence as they see their experiences mirrored in others, and they learn from each other as they hear a different take on the same questions. The facilitator's role is to ensure that every voice is heard, even in agreement with points already made. Each person's word choice and articulation are important.

Finally, ask each individual to craft a personal commitment based on their reflections and the group dialogue. These commitments should be shared in the group, enforcing the one team mindset, then be brought into ongoing 1:1 meetings, where you, as the leader, provide support, coaching, resources, and accountability.

This process transforms your team from observers of change into creators of it. They become decision makers and designers on the path through their commitments. This activity will also surface team norms or ways of working that must adjust, change, or be added in service of the aligned vision.

Collaboration Forums to Sustain Progress

You've set the vision and built ownership. Now comes the real work of embedding new behaviours, systems, and approaches. This is the stage where things often get hard as the initial energy fades and real challenges surface, and structured forums with your leadership presence become more important than ever.

I use collaboration forums to stay connected and build momentum. I recommend specific forums for specific intentions, so here are a few types and how best to use them:

- Weekly team check-ins are best for continued team alignment and progress reports on commitments.

- Open office hours can be leveraged for skill building or knowledge sharing. They are pointed to the expertise needed for what you are navigating, and a great space for guest speakers.

- Peer-to-peer working groups are ideal for issue resolution and problem solving, as more minds are better than one when working out the nuts and bolts of execution.

- Leadership "podcasts" or storytelling sessions can be used to recognize small wins that build momentum and share your perspective on what continues to give you confidence.

The format matters less than the intention. What's important is consistency, clarity, and your presence. Your team needs to feel you're in it with them—available to problem-solve, ready to celebrate wins, and willing to adjust course when needed.

These forums also give space for your early adopters to share stories, as their voices are powerful. Their small wins can build momentum through storytelling as they share ways they have overcome resistance and are seeing success. Consider giving them a microphone, literally, and let their experiences guide and inspire others.

The Leader's Role in a Volatile World

We live in a time of extraordinary volatility and change, a relentless work pace, and at times with an unclear path forward. However, as leaders, we have the opportunity to help others navigate today's world, and that is how we choose to show up during uncertainty and change.

We may not be able to control every circumstance—in fact, we cannot —but we can control our response and how we choose to lead with vision, with transparency, with empathy, and with curiosity. We can build trust through consistency, invite courage through collaboration, and foster growth by knowing others are capable. We just need to tap into it.

Your team is watching. They are listening and observing how you own decisions and, yes, how you own mistakes. They crave authenticity, are inspired through alignment, and can be empowered through co-creation and collaboration. So show up fully, invite others to join you, share vision, and build systems that empower others because you aren't just leading tasks and final execution against data and metrics, you are leading people who are capable of greatness.

I hope you have found a nugget or two to consider as you evolve your leadership approach, and if you would like to carry on the conversation, to go deeper on these topics or more on leading change, please reach out to me via LinkedIn. I am always happy to collaborate.

About the Author

Jen Robertson-Hatanaka is a seasoned executive leader and transformation strategist with over 25 years of experience guiding high-impact teams across retail, hospitality, and customer service sectors. Known for her people-first approach, Jen blends strategic insight with human-centered leadership to create inclusive cultures and drive meaningful change.

Her professional journey spans from barista to market-level VP and is a testament to the power of mentorship, curiosity, and an unwavering belief in what's possible. Along the way, Jen has championed operational excellence, scaled market strategies, and empowered countless individuals to unlock their own potential.

Outside of the boardroom, Jen is leading a very different kind of transformation: regenerating a 6.5-acre homestead on British Columbia's Sunshine Coast with her family. The project is a personal legacy—rooted in community, sustainability, and the joy of building something together.

A generous collaborator and natural coach, Jen is energized by supporting others in their leadership journey. She believes in the power of possibility, and that every individual brings unique talents worth discovering and celebrating. Whether you're looking to elevate your strategy, empower your teams, or simply brainstorm big ideas, Jen is ready to partner with you.

To connect with Jen and learn more about her work, visit www.linkedin.com/in/jen-robertson-hatanaka.

Chapter 8

Beyond Coaching: How My Business Found Its True Calling (and How Yours Can Too!)

By Paul Cecala, GCDF

I LOVE what I do! I am PASSIONATE about helping people find meaningful and fulfilling work that allows them to live the lifestyle they want! I absolutely love being a career coach! For the 10 years that I have been doing this full-time, I have not worked a single day, and I plan to do it for as long as I can. Notice also that I have not used the "J" word (job) once in that declaration! Why? Because I don't have a job. I do work that I love.

I also believe all of you should have that same love and passion for your work as I do for mine. At Cecala Career Consultants, LLC, that is what we do: help people find their passion and provide the project plan to get that work.

In this chapter, I want to pull back the curtain a bit on how my business became what it is today. I'm excited to share the **vision for my business** and how it's been evolving, because it exemplifies how you can build your passion into an income-generating business to sustain and expand your lifestyle choices. I hope to offer you insights that elevate and empower you, too.

Pivoting From Corporate America to Higher Education

But I am getting ahead of myself. Here is a bit more about how I came to be a solopreneur.

From my early teens, I always knew I liked to educate people, to share my knowledge and expertise, and see others grow and "become" based on what they learned. My professional career started in aviation sales. For me, sales was another word for, or way of, teaching people. I just happened to be teaching them about my products or services and why it was in their best interest to buy them. Toward the end of the 15 years in that field, I got cocky and took 2 roles that I was not prepared for. I got fired from them, which was devastating to my ego. Plus, in the 1990s, it was a very male-machismo-dominated field, and my need to live an authentic life as a gay man was clashing with the industry. It was time for a dramatic change.

When that career ended, I decided to pivot myself into higher education and teaching. But I did not have an advanced degree and no time or money to get one! Not willing to give up on what seemed like an ideal direction for my career, I sought out other ways to enter the industry and move into teaching.

What helped me make this decision was the guidance of a career coach who walked me through the job exploration process. I had done this once before in college when I realized being an astronaut or commercial pilot, while attainable goals at the time, were not careers

I was truly obsessed with. Flying was and is still an important avocation, just not something I want to do to make money.

Concurrently with looking for a new job, I fell in love with the job search process and now sought roles in career services. The keys to this career transition were:

1. Changing the way I spoke about my past positions using the terminology of the new industry and new role. For example, my products were graduates, and their features were the skills they learned.

2. Seeking a way to get my foot in the door (through career services) that would be a stepping stone to my ultimate goal of teaching.

3. Showing my knowledge, expertise, and passion for the new direction.

4. Carefully planning my transition. I needed to research the new industry, identify people I knew to network into it, explore different career paths, and develop the skills needed for success in those paths.

Business Takeaway: While making a pivot can be difficult, it can be done. It takes planning, intention, and learning how to speak to the new audience in a way that shows your value and expertise.

I have had several clients successfully pivot over the past decade. In each case, we identified the stepping stone positions they needed to accept along the way or the added skills they needed to obtain first. Then, using my job search project plan (see my book, *Take Control of*

Your Job Search, for more on that), we carefully identified their ideal employers, created a personal brand and marketing materials that cohesively told their story as an expert in the new field, and sent them to network with industry professionals who could assist in their search. Within 4-6 months, they landed.

From Solo Coach to Multi-faceted Group: The Big Shift

When I first waved goodbye to working for someone else and jumped into being a full-time solopreneur, my plan was pretty simple: just be a career coach. My goal was 5-6 hours a day of one-on-one coaching sessions, thinking that 25 hours a week would build a thriving, lucrative practice. That would leave 2 hours each day to do the stuff of running my business. Sounds great, right?

But, as many solo business owners quickly find out, the **reality of running a business** requires a lot more than 2 hours each day! Building a business takes far more marketing and advertising activities than I expected. Further, I did not understand the bookkeeping and legal issues I would need to handle. I suddenly realized that running the business of my business was going to take more time and brain power than I had allocated.

Maybe more precious than money is time. There are always ways to make more money. But time... once it passes, it's gone and you can never get it back. So, if I was to be successful, I needed to rapidly learn how to multiply my time or reduce the time I spent on non-income-generating activities like bookkeeping.

This is where having a good foundational business plan was helpful. By putting my ideas for the business in writing, the resulting goals solidified what I wanted to do and how I needed to do it to be successful. I had my blueprint for growth and success.

Business Takeaway: It is important to set realistic and achievable short-term goals while keeping the larger vision in mind. I now evaluate everything I do for its return on my investment of time and money. It is a balancing act, juggling several concurrent activities all designed to meet my business goals and objectives.

From Novice to Navigator: My Entrepreneurial Education

All the nitty-gritty aspects of a business hadn't factored into my grand plan until I started working with some fantastic business coaches. I needed to get smart about marketing and sales, technology and software, bookkeeping and accounting, contract writing and legal advice, business planning, and goal setting. I knew I had entry-level skills in these areas, but I realized I needed to at least become intermediately, if not expertly, skilled in them. If I couldn't become an expert, I needed to hire people who were!

I started small. I leaned on the skills I had and created tools that cost nothing to build. For example, my first customer relationship management system was an Excel spreadsheet from my best-selling job search workbook, *Take Control of Your Job Search*. When it could no longer manage my growing needs, I switched to a free online CRM allowing email blasts, sorting contacts for targeted marketing, and a whole lot more!

Later, when other homegrown tools became cumbersome, I invested in other software packages like QuickBooks, which really streamlined things. I leverage AI as a writing assistant, helping me brainstorm ideas and refine drafts for my blogs, articles, and books, which significantly boosts my efficiency. Eventually, I even hired a social media and marketing organization to help boost my SEO and get my marketing out there more prominently.

Business Takeaway: Use the experts around you for your own education and to maximize your time. I started with the things I knew best and sought out experts who would teach me what I didn't know. When appropriate, I hired those experts to take it to the next level. After two years in business, I could afford an upstart social media expert to improve my content and SEO. As I grew, my relationship with her company has grown too. After three years and difficulty in getting the right information to my accountant, I hired a bookkeeper for just one hour per month—that's all I need—to balance my bank accounts and fix my ledger entries.

Growing Pains, Growing Gains: New Streams of Income

As my business grew, I realized that 25 hours of one-on-one coaching might not be attainable, and my income was limited by time. My core goal of offering top-notch career guidance remained, but I began to diversify my offerings.

At the recommendation of my mentor, I added public speaking and keynote addresses, which not only bring in revenue but also boost brand awareness and offer a preview of my coaching services. I'm currently doing about four engagements monthly, sharing my expertise with diverse audiences, including well-received presentations at the annual conference of cybersecurity professionals (SECON 2025), the semi-annual PMI-NJ Career Fairs (Project Management Professionals), and other events.

Several of my trusted fellow coaches shared that their financial success included a high-revenue, low-time-commitment service. After considering a variety of options, last year I added **corporate training** to the mix. Recognizing the need for soft skills among new leaders, I developed practical courses in communications, customer relations, sales, leadership, and management skills to help today's professionals shine in their emerging leadership roles, all containing practical, pragmatic, and actionable steps attendees can take immediately to improve their effectiveness. Clients have already had me back for more courses because the first one went so well!

Finally, I wanted something that would provide passive (or, residual) income. Plus, I needed something to give me instant expert status. My second book, *Take Control of Your Job Search,* was the solution. With the help of a great publisher (Suzanne Doyle-Ingram and Prominence Publishing), it became an Amazon Best Seller in its category for three weeks, and https://bookauthority.org named it the second-best new read in its category for 2024. It continues to attract new clients, create opportunities to speak, build my brand, and create added revenue.

Business Takeaway: Don't be afraid to expand beyond your core competencies and initial vision. While my first love is one-on-one coaching, these new services allow me to spread my message farther and wider, reaching more people with less effort. And they generate more income. Ultimately, they give me the time and resources to do more coaching.

Cecala Career Consultants Today: A Multi-Faceted Approach

It takes effort to keep up with any industry; coaching is no different. I must constantly network with other coaches and be involved in my industry's professional association(s). Knowing what other coaches are doing, especially those I aspire to, keeps me current. It also helps me stay ahead of my closest competitors and elevates my professional skills significantly. Based on this "research" or industry intelligence, I am adjusting my offerings, knowledge, and style, which makes me a better coach.

Here is what Cecala Career Consultants currently offers:

- One-on-one career and leadership coaching

- Public speaking and keynote presentations

- Corporate training in leadership, communications, sales, and management skills

- My books, *Take Control of Your Job Search*, and *Work Search Buddies*

- And coming soon (currently in production!): A series of online tutorials to supplement the book!

My website, Version 2.0, was launched in the spring of 2025 to enhance its branding, better display my services and products, and pave the way for a future online store and subscription services.

Business Takeaway: To remain a leader in my field, I continue watching the competition, learning from other similar industries, and am open to new and diverse ways of doing business while ALWAYS keeping my primary vision and core business at the forefront. I am not afraid to pivot to a new direction if it supports my primary vision. Doing so has made me a respected thought leader among career coaches and helped my business grow.

I recently worked with two software developers who were laid off—not uncommon in the IT industry these days. Scott sought out a role coding in the same language he had been coding for the last eight years, as he did not know any other programming language. It took him nearly nine months to find a new position, and it was just a six-month contract.

Elizabeth, expecting she would ultimately need a new job, learned AWS and Python while working. When she was laid off, she quickly took and completed a course in AI programming. She was hired in just four months for a long-term position, and the employer adjusted her workday to finish the AI course. She reported that keeping up-to-date and advancing her skills was what got her the job.

In today's ultra-fast-paced business environment with revolutionary technology coming at you seemingly every few years, it is critical that you are always learning, always networking, and always adapting. You need to get ahead just to keep up, or you will be left behind.

The "Aha!" Moment: Why I Love What I Do

A huge key to my personal success and enjoyment is that all of these are areas where I truly excel, and more importantly, **I LOVE doing them!** Seeing that "Aha!" moment on my clients' faces when they "get it" is absolutely exhilarating.

Yesterday, I suggested to a client that they approach their job search as a B2B sales process. You could literally see the bulb light up in his brain as his face went from fear and stress to understanding and excitement. He said, "Paul, you are blowing my mind with that perspective! This will revolutionize the way I am approaching my career!" And that makes it all worthwhile. Since embarking on this journey, I truly haven't felt like I've "worked" a day. I've just been doing the things I love to do, with people I love to work with!

You can tell my coaching strategy tends to be pragmatic, practical, and tactical. We will quickly identify the issues, design a personalized project plan to address them, and then get right to attacking those concerns with actionable steps moving you forward to your goal every single day.

Like so many other clients, Sarah, a recent graduate starting her career, commented, "I really appreciate how you listen to what I am saying and then offer guidance specific to my concerns. After talking to you for just a few sessions, I feel like we are long-time friends and confidants."

I would genuinely love to hear your stories of "finding and growing your passion." Additionally, if you need a hand figuring out your passion or how to grow your business, let me know. Cecala Career Consultants, LLC, can help you make it happen! Together, let's elevate your career and empower you to be more than you ever thought possible.

About the Author

Known as the project planning career coach, Paul Cecala is a two-time author of job search books, a certified Global Career Development Facilitator, and founder of Cecala Career Consultants, LLC. He has assisted over 4000 job seekers, from C-suite executives to college students, to find work they are passionate about.

Paul's first book, Take Control of Your Job Search, is an Amazon's Best Seller, and was named the #2 Best New Read in its Category for 2024 by www.bookauthority.org. People have been commenting on the high quality of the step-by-step worksheets defining how to conduct an effective job search.

Paul specializes in creating job search project plans and is known for his empathetic listening skills. He has been praised for networking skills, interview techniques, and resume writing. He has assisted people from a variety of backgrounds with expertise in DEI&B, aviation, business, project management, technology (IT/IS and Fin Tech), pharma/biotech, healthcare, and more.

Paul facilitates job seeker networking groups for four different organizations. He has helmed the adult professional education programs for two colleges and a NJ Dept. of Labor One-Stop Career Center.

Prior to career coaching, he spent 15 years in corporate aviation sales with industry leading organizations ending as Vice President of Aircraft Charter Sales.

Paul has his BS in Psychology from Florida Institute of Technology. Besides his two books, he has authored numerous articles on career coaching in a variety of online and print publications.

Chapter 9

The Exit—What Success Looks Like

By Tony Beebe

Smoke curled from the cigarette as the owner signed the papers and joked about heading to his favorite bar to celebrate. Right to the end, he smoked in the office like it was on the set of Dallas in the 1980s.

Another founder threw a blowout party in New York, renting out a floor in Rockefeller Center and hiring Harry Connick Jr. and the Rockettes to celebrate his birthday and the sale of his company. One vanished to a quiet California beach for time with family. One stayed put—same house, same friends, same truck—just fewer phone calls. And one? He was already scheming the next big one.

For most founders, selling their company feels like the grand finale— the check, the toast, the moment when all the hard work finally pays off. But after working with dozens of them, I've learned something else entirely: Selling isn't the end. It's the turning point. It reveals who you are, what really matters, and what comes next. Every founder writes their ending.

As an advisor, I had to meet them wherever they were—no script, no playbook, just real life. Each story came with its curveballs. I stayed ready, listened closely, and stepped in where it mattered most.

I grew up in rural Iowa and went to high school and college in Florida, where I earned an engineering degree and raced cars on the weekends. My wife, two sons, and I live in Houston, Texas. I'm active in scouting and love being outdoors, whether hiking, camping, or simply taking in the fresh air.

I started my career offshore—working as a roughneck to a driller—on rigs around the world. Then came management roles, business school for an MBA, and eventually C-level positions. I took a company public, co-founded an offshore drilling firm, helped raise $1.4 billion, and scaled the business to 400 people as COO and interim CFO. Along the way, I've lived in 12 countries, worked in 21, and traveled to 55. Sometimes I feel like a local everywhere and a nomad all at once. But Texas? That's home.

Since then, I've served as an angel investor, board member, and advisor, helping founders sell their companies and partnering with the private equity firms that buy them. I've sat through tough earnout negotiations and coached owners through the hardest question of all:

What does success mean to me?

It's rarely just the money. More often, it's about legacy, team, identity, or family. Sometimes it's a chip on the shoulder, or the freedom to finally let something go.

This isn't a step-by-step strategy guide. Instead, I'll share three stories—each with its own lesson—because every founder I've met has carved a unique path, paid a price few outsiders can truly grasp, and discovered that grit, self-awareness, and purpose matter far more than any playbook ever could. You'll see three radically different outcomes, each shaped by founders navigating high-stakes decisions in real time, under pressure, with no safety net or second chance.

They taught me lessons I still carry with me. Maybe they'll do the same for you.

Story 1—The Marine

Lesson One: Know when to pass the reins.

Pete was a Marine who went on to become an entrepreneur and build a successful business. For years, his instincts made him a legend—until the game changed, and instinct wasn't enough.

Construction is a brutal business, and Pete, a Marine from Odessa, Texas, made it his arena. Drafted during Vietnam, he manned a machine gun in a helicopter. When he came home, he took a job at an electrical supply company, but one muddy job site changed everything.

He watched the crew rig up thick power cables—over an inch in diameter, with a copper core and heavily insulated—spooling them out and pulling them by hand through overhead trays. Each cable could weigh up to five pounds per foot, and the crews often dragged 300 to 400 feet at a time through a maze of steel, equipment, and obstacles. It was backbreaking work, and then Pete saw the markup on the invoice.

That moment stuck with him.

He called some old Marine buddies. "We've done harder in worse places," he told them. And just like that, the business was born—gritty, loyal, and lean.

Throughout the 1980s and 2000s, Pete built a mini-empire. He bought out competitors, expanded into new regions, and established a brand that people recognized and respected. At his peak, the rumor was that he cleared over a million dollars a month.

In the 2010s, we prepared for an exit. Pete brought in another Marine to assist in managing the sale. I was hired to oversee operations across the group, comprising three companies, 800 employees, and numerous moving parts. I streamlined systems, improved margin visibility, and helped stabilize three integrated businesses.

Pete's companies had a distinct vibe. Every office was chosen so he could smoke indoors, even in the 2010s. Chain-smoking was the norm, and two smokers could fog up a private jet cabin in minutes. Dipping was just as common—guys kept tobacco tucked in their lips, with Solo cups or empty bottles always nearby so they didn't have to spit on the floor. It wasn't a polished culture, but it was loyal, fast-moving, and built on trust.

Margins were razor-thin. With lean systems, smart hires, and acquisitions, we increased their market share from low single digits to 23%.

That's when private equity made its appearance.

One firm offered to take us public overnight, through a SPAC—and we did. We worked through diligence, legal wrangling, and investor roadshows. Pete joined part of the pitch, but the New York investors didn't quite get him, and he didn't get them.

He hadn't hunted since Vietnam, said he'd done enough killing for a lifetime there.

At one meeting, I sat at the end of the table—the head seats were reserved for egos. To my left: polished shoes and impeccably groomed titans of finance—pressed shirts, tailored slacks, luxury watches, and precisely trimmed nose hair, ears, and eyebrows. To my right: sunburned, bearded men with calloused hands, untrimmed hair, Carhartt jackets, Red Wing boots, and worn Wranglers cinched with scuffed belt buckles.

Both sides thought they were tough. But only one had manned a machine gun in a helicopter over the jungle.

Pete didn't say much in New York, but you could feel him in the room. He might not have had an MBA or worn Italian loafers, but he was the toughest guy at the table. And the only one who didn't need to prove it.

We closed the deal. Pete walked away with an eight-figure check. Spirits were high. We identified a new market segment with significant contracts and no dominant player. With the board's backing, we launched a new division to pursue it.

And that's when we made the mistake.

A salesman overheard bar talk in Mexico: competitors were underbidding. Pete, always the closer, trusted his gut and slashed our bid.

We won the bid. Each project was valued at $180 million, with an expected profit of approximately $14 million. However, since the client paid only 75% upon delivery, we had to borrow heavily to fund the construction. The interest alone was $22 million per project, wiping out all profit and putting us $8 million in the red. With numbers like that, no bank would finance it. We were underwater before we even started.

Footnote to Self: If the CEO slashes the bid, don't let financing costs vanish from the spreadsheet. It turns out that banks like to get paid.

Compounding the problem, our business was cyclical, and it turned. Bankers got spooked. Capital dried up. One even joked that they would restrict funds so Pete wouldn't buy a new jet if they financed it.

Pete pushed to raise more capital, but the market wasn't there this time. The nine-figure dream faded. What was left became a cautionary tale. We eventually sold the company in the downturn.

It wasn't the ending Pete deserved, but he'd gotten an eight-figure check earlier. Unfortunately, the company didn't make it to the next level.

Lesson 1: Know when to pass the reins. Pete got paid, but if he had stepped away, he'd have secured the win; instead, staying too long cost him the upside he'd earned. What built the company couldn't carry it forward, and knowing the difference is everything.

Story 2—The Charmer

Lesson 2: Charisma can open doors, but it can't build the company.

Some people just have it—that grin, that spark, that undeniable pull. Arnold had it.

Arnold was a balding, overweight Brit with a dirty sense of humor and magnetic charm. He pitched me a data analytics startup aimed at the oilfield, and I grilled him hard—after all, I'd run billion-dollar projects. This wasn't a place for fluff. But Arnold didn't bluff. His questions were sharp, his answers even sharper—and I remembered him.

We didn't buy the software, but I stayed in touch. A few months later, Arnold had emptied his 401(k), mortgaged his house, and recruited a team—a Scottish business developer, an ex-Army captain, and a pack of believers chasing the vision.

When he raised a friends-and-family round, I joined. His charisma was real and contagious. He landed two global oil clients. A California VC joined next. At its peak, the team had 80 employees and a $34 million valuation.

Then things took a turn.

In the middle of pandemic-era fundraising, the CFO quit to marry a younger woman and drive cross-country in a vintage RV. Yes, that actually happened. I stepped in as interim CFO to help close the Series B3, chasing term sheets while he chased sunsets. I secured bridge funding, rebuilt confidence with the board, and closed the raise.

In the meeting, when Arnold asked me to become the interim CFO at a British Pub, he got the waitress's number mid-order. He never called her, just liked the exchange. So did she. Arnold was a world-class fundraiser—better at selling stock than software. He genuinely cared about his team, many of whom were single moms he'd recruited personally and mentored. But two blind spots emerged, each more costly than Arnold realized, especially for someone with so much natural instinct.

The first was with the board.

He once confided in me that he believed his job was to argue, push for his position, challenge every suggestion, and keep the board at arm's length. But by turning every issue into a hill to die on, he gradually eroded their goodwill. And these weren't just investors—they were also our largest customers.

The second was with our key client in Europe.

Between pandemic travel restrictions and his belief that the customer success team had it under control, Arnold never made the trip. He didn't call. He didn't nurture the spark that had initially won the client's trust. And as frustrations built, no one escalated the issue. The customer drifted away. Sales hiring exploded while product execution slipped. The pilot concluded without a follow-on contract. Confidence eroded, and the board began to lose faith.

The board pushed for layoffs of 75%. Arnold pushed back, and they tried harder. He stopped listening. Eventually, he was replaced, and the Army Captain took over as CEO. The company sold not long after. It wasn't a home run, but it wasn't a zero either. What still held value was Arnold himself: his story, his brand, and that spark you couldn't fake.

Today, Arnold chairs a new company—but this time, he has seasoned operators by his side. He's still the spark, but now he knows when to hand off the flamethrower.

Maybe success isn't always yachts and champagne. Sometimes, it's surviving the storm and turning a dog's breakfast into a Sunday roast.

Lesson 2: Charisma opens doors. But systems, strategy, and self-awareness keep them open.

Story 3—Life Day

Lesson 3: Success isn't the size of the exit. It's what you do with the time it gives you.

We had just closed a small SaaS acquisition with sharp founders, clean code, and a tight team. A few weeks later, I found myself in a glass-walled conference room, reviewing integration plans with the two founders. Then Matt glanced at the silent TV in the corner—live police chase, helicopters overhead, flashing lights below.

"That's David's office," one of them said.

His partner leaned in. "That's David's landlord. He just shot him."

I turned. "David?"

"Yeah. David. The guy you tried to buy last year."

The words hit like a jolt.

David ran a SaaS platform that optimized machine performance. I had led the acquisition efforts a while back, drawn by their strong product, recurring revenue, and solid team. We couldn't agree on valuation, though, so we shook hands and walked away with mutual respect, but no deal.

And now? He'd been shot. On Valentine's Day.

The landlord had walked through the office, handing roses to each employee. When he got to David, he gave him a rose, then pulled a pistol and fired. Somehow, David survived. It wasn't about rent. Technically, it was a lease dispute. But really—how do you even process something like that?

Weeks later, I called him. The business had taken a hit. David was still recovering, physically and emotionally. The team was shaken, and resources were tight. But here's what stuck with me: He didn't just survive. He attacked his recovery.

The bullet had shattered the upper row of teeth on one side of his mouth. The impact likely saved his life, but it meant more than a dozen reconstructive surgeries. Eighteen, I think. His jaw, teeth, and nerves were rebuilt piece by piece. He couldn't eat solid foods for months, so he made healthy smoothies. Every day. His family pitched in—blending in, cheering, and turning a medical marathon into a mission.

That initial call led to a meeting—and eventually, my first angel investment. I helped him rebuild the company's financial foundation while he rebuilt himself. By the time he returned to public life, he wasn't just healed. He was transformed.

At industry events, he took the stage like a man reborn—channeling Steve Jobs in his black sweater, but with a smile you couldn't fake. To my knowledge, he never told anyone about the events, but it was well known, and people would ask him about it.

And here's the wild part: After being shot in the face, the man negotiated better than most lawyers I've met. Go figure.

Six months later, we sold to a private equity firm. Four months after that, it was sold again to a strategic buyer. It was a solid outcome, but the mechanics of the deal weren't what made it memorable. David did. He negotiated every term like a pro. But he'd changed.

During his recovery, he told me he'd been asking himself the hard questions. Why had he worked so relentlessly? What was it really for? His answer surprised me with its clarity: Family. Friends. Freedom.

He still negotiated hard, but this time, he was willing to compromise just enough to get it done. The exit gave him financial security—and something more: time. Time to live. Time with his kids. Time to be present.

Years later, his son told me something that stuck with me: They no longer call it Valentine's Day.

"We call it Life Day," he said. "It's the day everything could've ended, but didn't."

In business, we talk about wins in multiples, timing, and exits, but the best outcomes aren't always the biggest—they're the most meaningful.

Lesson 3: The best exits don't just make you rich. They give you freedom to live.

Closing—Founder Success

When founders sell, it's as emotional as sending a child to college, walking a daughter down the aisle, or watching a son go off to war.

One was a Marine who built something big and learned Wall Street doesn't care how tough you are when the cycle turns.

One rode his charm far—but not far enough to outrun burnout, weak systems, and the limits we all face eventually.

One got shot in the face—on Valentine's Day—and lived to rebuild a business and a life.

These aren't just stories about EBITDA or exits. They're about the part that spreadsheets can't measure: the founder. The grit. The fire. The sacrifices are made when no one is watching.

Every founder has flaws. Every single one. But they've also paid a heavy price—a price that shaped them into who they are. They've had to grow, learn, and manage fear and risk in ways that most people will never experience. And when they come through it? They often emerge with something more profound: purpose, direction, and a kind of earned confidence that only comes from being self-made.

The middle is always messy—false starts, tough calls, and the daily challenge of waking up stronger than whatever lies ahead. That's what makes success real.

Three simple lessons:

1. Get paid, but know that instincts built in private companies don't always translate to public companies.

2. Charisma opens doors, but strategy and discipline keep them open.

3. Time is the best return—use it well.

Because the truth is, every founder finishes their journey on their terms, or not at all. There's no script. No formula. Just the unique path carved by your experiences as a founder.

These days, I work with founders at the crossroads. Some want to scale. Others are ready to step away. Some need a successor who will honor what they've built. Others just want help cleaning up a spreadsheet their niece made eight years ago. I'm here for all of it. And honestly, helping a founder write the final chapter—or helping the buyer start the first—is the best part of my job. I've been through exits, near-misses, and full-on fire drills with founders. If you're in it now, I'll stand beside you—whether we're closing a deal or dodging bullets.

It's worth it. Just try not to get shot in the face.

And if you've already exited? Tell me your story. Let's celebrate what success really looks like—flawed, hard-fought, and absolutely worth it. There's no perfect script. Just your version of what success looks like. And if yours includes a yacht, a beach, or a bar tab the size of a Series A... well, that counts too.

About the Author

Tony Beebe is an advisor, investor, and executive coach who helps founders exit well, partners with private equity to buy and grow businesses, and guides executives through high-stakes transitions. His 30-year career spans 55 countries and more roles than he ever planned for—COO, CFO, board member, founder, and a few seats in economy class.

After earning his engineering degree (and later an MBA), Tony chose offshore drilling rigs over corner offices—he wanted to understand how things really worked before building them. From roughneck to driller to global executive, he's led major projects in 21 countries, co-founded companies, taken one public via SPAC, raised over $1.4 billion, and holds three patents in marine technology.

Today, Tony runs an advisory practice focused on helping founders and owners scale their businesses, prepare for exit, or sell their companies. He partners with private equity firms to identify, acquire, and grow the right businesses, bringing operational insight and strategic alignment to every deal. He also speaks at conferences and panels, sharing stories that blend grit, global perspective, and just enough dry humor to keep it interesting.

He knows what it's like on both sides of the table.

He's open to select keynotes, podcasts, and M&A collaborations—especially if there's good coffee, curious people, or a deal worth building. If you're exploring a sale, recap, growth investment, or exit strategy, let's talk.

Tony serves on multiple boards and volunteers with Scouts. He lives in Houston with his wife and two sons.

Connect with Tony on LinkedIn:
https://www.linkedin.com/in/tony-beebe/

Chapter 10

Why Your Story Matters (And Why the World Needs to Hear It)

By Gregg Gonzales

I grew up believing that storytelling was something reserved for "other people." You know the ones—the writers with glasses perched precariously on their noses, furiously typing away on a vintage typewriter in a Paris café; or the polished keynote speakers who could step on stage and command a crowd with a perfect anecdote that tied together laughter, tears, and a call to action in fifteen minutes flat.

That wasn't me. At least, not then.

I was the guy who thought stories were something you consumed through books, movies, family gatherings, or maybe over a rare campfire. Definitely not something you were responsible for telling yourself! My life was filled with stories, but they were tucked away, silently waiting for me to give them a voice that I didn't know I had.

Over the course of my life, I learned that storytelling isn't just a nice-to-have skill. It's not just for writers or speakers or "creative types." It's the center-point and heartbeat of **true human connection**. It's how we remember, how we relate, and how we understand ourselves in the chaos of a fast-moving, noisy, and often disconnected world.

And the most important realization I had? YOUR story matters. MY story matters. EVERY SINGLE STORY MATTERS! Not because it's epic or captivating or because it will end up on the *New York Times* bestseller list, but because the act of sharing your story is how you discover who you are, connect with others, and create impact in ways you can't predict.

That's why I created The SpeakEasy Method—a way to help people tell their stories with clarity, courage, and true authenticity. Over the course of this chapter, I want to show you why storytelling is your secret superpower, especially in business, leadership (and life!), and how to start using it in a way that's powerful, deeply human, and EASY!

The Myth of the Perfect Story

When I first started helping people tell their stories, I noticed something interesting. Almost everyone I started working with believed their story wasn't good enough.

"Who would care about this?" they'd say. "My story isn't that special. Nothing happened to me that would inspire anyone or make a difference."

This is the myth of the "perfect story." The idea that only extraordinary lives produce extraordinary stories. But here's the truth: Stories aren't about perfection, they're about **connection**. Think about the stories that move you most. It's rarely the ones where everything went perfectly. It's usually the ones where someone failed, stumbled, and then figured something out along the way.

Perfection isn't relatable. Humanity is.

That's why your story (even the awkward, unfinished, imperfect parts) carries weight. Because when you share it, you give people permission to see themselves in you. In that moment, you're not just telling a story. You're creating a bridge.

Storytelling in Business: More Than a Buzzword

Now, let's talk about business.

For years, "storytelling" has been tossed around as a buzzword in marketing departments and leadership seminars. Everyone nods along when someone says, "Storytelling is key!" but few know how to actually do it without sounding cliché.

Here's what I've seen: In business, people often hide behind jargon, data, and "professionalism." They worry that if they share too much of themselves, they won't be taken seriously. So they fill presentations with bullet points, charts, and industry terms that are technically accurate, but emotionally lifeless.

The problem? Facts inform, but stories TRANSFORM.

Imagine two people pitching the same idea. One rattles off numbers, market trends, and growth forecasts. The other begins with a personal story:

"Two years ago, I stood in my kitchen staring at a medical bill I couldn't pay. That's when I realized there had to be a better way to handle healthcare costs. That's why I built this company..."

Which one are you leaning in to hear more from? Stories cut through noise. They create emotional buy-in. They make the complex simple and the ordinary memorable, and in business, where trust is currency and relationships drive results, storytelling isn't just nice; it's necessary.

The SpeakEasy Method: Unlocking Your Story

So, how do you actually tell your story in a way that works, whether that's through a book, in business, on a stage, or even across the dinner table?

That's where my approach comes in: The SpeakEasy Method.

Here's the quick version. The SpeakEasy Method is built on four core pillars:

1. **Curiosity**: Start with questions. Your story lives in the questions you're willing to ask yourself. Who am I? What moments shaped me? Where did I stumble, and what did I learn? Curiosity cracks the door open.

2. **Attention**: The best stories hold attention, not just because of what's said, but how it's said. Attention is about presence—being fully engaged with your audience and the story itself. It's noticing when the energy shifts, when a laugh lands, when silence deepens. It's about crafting your story in a way that

invites people in and keeps them leaning forward, curious about what comes next.

3. **Connection**: Storytelling isn't about performance; it's about relationships. When you tell your story, you're not broadcasting; it's a conversation. You're creating space for someone else to see themselves in what you share.

4. **Clarity**: A great story doesn't need to be long or complicated. It needs to be clear. What's the moment? What's the change? What's the takeaway? That's all you need.

Why Your Story Matters (Even When You Think It Doesn't)

One of my favorite moments in workshops is when someone says, "But my story isn't important," and then they share something small, like how their grandmother always saved the crusts from sandwiches, or the time they got lost on the way to school and found their way home. Everyone else in the room? Captivated.

Here's why: Stories aren't about scale, they're about resonance.

Think of it like music. A song doesn't have to be loud to move you. It just has to hit the right note. Your story, whether it's about launching a business, surviving a heartbreak, or just making it through Tuesday, is a note someone else needs to hear, because when they hear it, they'll realize they're not alone.

Humor: The Secret Ingredient

Here's another nugget I want to share with you: Humor is the duct tape of storytelling. It fixes almost anything. Now, I don't mean you need to turn your story into a stand-up routine (unless that's your thing), but sprinkling in humor does two important things:

1. It puts your audience at ease.

2. It reminds them that you (and they) are human.

When I first started speaking, I was always trying to be so serious. I thought every story had to be profound and moving, every sentence dripping with wisdom and insight. But people don't want to be lectured. They want to laugh AND learn.

So now, when I tell stories, I share the embarrassing moments too. Like the time I completely blanked in the middle of a speech and ended up talking about my love of New Mexican food for five minutes straight! (Spoiler: People remembered the New Mexico cuisine story more than my actual content.)

Humor makes your story extra sticky, because when people laugh, they listen.

Bringing It All Together: Your Story in Action

So what does this all mean for you, especially if you're using storytelling in business, leadership, or life? Here's the roadmap:

1. **Start small.** You don't need a TED Talk. Start by telling a story at your next dinner gathering or in your next team meeting. Share something real, something human.

2. **Lead with vulnerability**. Share a failure, a lesson, a mistake. That's where connection lives.

3. **Tie it to meaning**. Every story should answer the question: "Why does this matter to me right now?"

4. **Practice in safe spaces**. Tell your story to a friend, colleague, or coach before you tell it on stage. (Shameless plug: This is exactly what I help people do with the SpeakEasy Method!)

5. **Repeat, and repeat again.** The more you tell your story, the clearer it gets.

Storytelling isn't a one-time thing. It's a practice—like a muscle that needs strengthening—and the more you use it, the stronger and more powerful it gets.

The World Needs Your Story

If you take nothing else from this chapter, let it be this: **The world needs your story**. Not the polished, perfect, all-wrapped-up version. The real one. The messy one. The one that still makes your voice shake a little when you share it. Your story is how you connect. It's how you lead. It's how you build trust, spark change, and leave a legacy. And maybe, just maybe, it's the exact story someone else needs to hear to take the next step in their own journey. So don't wait. Don't tell yourself it doesn't matter. Don't hide behind data, or busyness, or fear.

Speak easily. Speak proudly. Speak truthfully.

Because your story isn't just yours; it's a gift for the rest of the world, too.

About the Author

Gregg Gonzales is the founder of *The SpeakEasy Method*. He is a story producer and teacher who has helped hundreds of people bring their stories to life. He leads seminars, workshops and retreats that blend storytelling with connection, creating spaces where voices are heard and communities grow.

His vision is to raise awareness around brain health while strengthening human connection globally. He currently lives in Denver, Colorado.

Connect with Gregg on LinkedIn:

https://www.linkedin.com/in/gregg-gonzales-speakeasy0622

or visit his website at www.thespeakeasymethod.co

Conclusion

You have just walked through ten rooms in the same house, each offering a key, a story, and a next step. The pattern is intentional: personal truth drives professional traction, and small, consistent actions compound. Leadership, in the end, is as much inner work as it is outer results.

Now it is your turn to keep the momentum going. Choose one practice from one chapter and live with it for the next seven days. Put it on your calendar. Tell a colleague what you are trying and ask them to check in with you. At the end of the week, keep what worked, adjust what did not, and choose the next practice to test.

If you lead a team, bring an idea from this book into your next meeting. Five minutes is enough. Ask one question that opens a real conversation. Listen fully. Capture the actions you hear and commit to one small move together. Culture changes through a series of clear, honest moments like that.

A few simple thoughts can help you revisit this book with fresh eyes:

- What did I learn about the way I think, decide, and show up?

- What small change would create an outsized result this month?

- Who needs to hear one of these ideas from me today?

Before you close the cover, consider reaching out to the authors on LinkedIn or through their websites. They are real people who made time to share what they have learned, and they would truly appreciate hearing which idea helped you. You could send a short note with one takeaway or result you tried. A simple message like, "Your chapter helped me do X this week. Thank you," can make their day and often starts a valuable conversation.

Come back to these chapters when change happens or things feel unsure. Different lines will stand out at different times because you will be a different leader each time you return. That is the gift of a book like this. It stays with you.

www.ingramcontent.com/pod-product-compliance
Lightning Source LLC
Chambersburg PA
CBHW062023200326
41519CB00017B/4908